BEYOND THE HORIZON

JEAN PRESTON

WESTBOW
PRESS®
A DIVISION OF THOMAS NELSON
& ZONDERVAN

WestBow Press books may be ordered through booksellers or by contacting:

WestBow Press
A Division of Thomas Nelson & Zondervan
1663 Liberty Drive
Bloomington, IN 47403
www.westbowpress.com
844-714-3454

ISBN: 978-1-6642-3341-6 (sc)
ISBN: 978-1-6642-3340-9 (e)

Print information available on the last page.

WestBow Press rev. date: 06/16/2021

PART I

Journey into the Unknown

CHAPTER 1

How quickly darkness falls when sunset is already shrouded by heavy rain clouds down on the last rays of light. So like depression edging out the light and threatening to overwhelm the soul with its pervasive insistence, pulling the blackout curtains across the window, Florence shrugged her shoulders and moved across the room to shut off the radio.

The BBC news gave plenty of cause for alarm. The Germans were stepping up their bombing raids on Britain already reeling from two years of bombardments on cities, railways, and docks. What if Germany were to win the war? Would the brutality of the Nazis spill out into the British streets? The news was getting increasingly frightening and evacuation orders had forced many families to send their children to the countryside for safekeeping.

Glancing down at her baby Jean sleeping peacefully in the crib she felt thankful that she had been able to keep her with her. If they were going to die they would both go together. She had moved back home to be with her mother and sisters after her husband Ron had been called up by the military and sent overseas. She had no idea where they had sent him.

The front door burst open and her sisters came in all chattering noisily about their work at the factory and the new spitfire aircraft that were on line. Startled, her baby started crying and added to their raised voices. She clamped her hands over her ears and tried to calm her baby Jean who was now in full flow with her own cries. It was all too much.

"Please," she said, "just all quiet down and we can catch up with each other's news over dinner." Lola and Gladys headed for the kitchen as Evelyn took over the now smiling baby while Florence went into the front room to check on their mother. To make her mother aware of her presence, Florence touched her gently on the shoulder. The morphine had helped and she had slept soundly all day. "Can you eat something, Mum? It may make you feel a little better." Her mother shook her head.

Cancer had ravaged her body and she had no desire to eat.

"No," she said. "Just give me some more pain medication so that I can go back to sleep." Florence brought a glass of water and gave her some pills. Doing her best to make her mother comfortable, she plumped up her pillows, gave her a kiss, and then went out to join her sisters at the dinner table. As they ate they all discussed the latest news, only causing them to continue to worry. This war seemed to be going on forever with no end in sight.

They were starting to wash the dishes when the shrieking sound of an air raid siren came, shattering nerves and causing them all to feel a sense of dread. They felt this whenever an air raid was imminent. Due to their mother's condition, none of them would seek the relative security of an air raid shelter. Her pain was too agonizing for her to be moved from her bed. Evelyn went to sit with her and the others headed for the staircase... it was the next safest place to be in an air raid. They soon heard the drone of aircraft engines moving overhead as they huddled together on the staircase praying silently. Bombs were exploding all around them.

Florence heard a whining noise seconds before the others. She screamed, "This one is for us," as she leaned over her baby to protect her, but her voice was lost in the noise and falling debris. Blackness closed in around her. ......

CHAPTER 2

J ean blew out the candles on her birthday cake. She was excited and happy to be 6 years old. She closed her eyes and made a secret wish. Everyone sang "Happy Birthday" to her and she felt very important. Her mother and aunts were all there although Grandma didn't come with them to live at an Uncle's house after the bombing.

They said that Grandma had gone to heaven. She didn't know where that was, but it sounded like a very happy place. She knew about the heavenly Father that her mother told her about in her prayers, but she couldn't see him either. She wished that her father would come back. She tried to imagine what he would look like. She pictured a soldier, strong and handsome, but couldn't see his face. That night after her mother tucked her into bed she whispered her secret wish into her rag doll's ear…. she always told her about her wishes and she always kept her secrets.

Sleeping soundly she was suddenly woken up when her mother switched on the light and shook her. "Wake up, Jean there is exciting news! The war has finally ended and everyone is going out into the street to celebrate. We don't want to miss this it will be a time to remember all our lives." They ran together down the stairs and outside into the cold night air. People were streaming out of their houses shouting and singing and crowds were gathering together and dancing. A group danced by them doing the "Hokey Cokey" and pulled them along into the line. There were cheers and tears of joyful voices rang out singing the war has ended and we have won. Strangers were hugging each other and a group nearby started to sing "God Save Our Gracious King." So many joined in and others sang "Jerusalem". Church bells rang out all over the country spreading the wonderful news. At daybreak people started to go back to their homes and the streets slowly emptied again. The celebration ended, but the memory was one that Jean would never forget.

Two weeks later as Florence was getting breakfast there was a rattle of the letter box and a loud knock on the door. A postman stood outside and handed her a telegram. Her heart sank. Was this bad news? Surely her husband hadn't been injured or worse yet been killed right at the end of the war? She took it inside and sat down. Taking a deep breath she slowly opened it and the words gradually sank in.… Ron was alive and well and had decided to take a job in East Africa. He had arranged for her and Jean to come and join him and had booked a passage for them on a troop ship called the Antenor. This ship was taking troops back to their countries. The final destination was Mombasa in Kenya. She stood up dropping the telegram on the floor, tears welled up in her eyes, her mind racing in a thousand different directions. A new life in a faraway country - could this be possible after all these terrible years of war? Leaving it all behind would be so good, but leaving her sisters and family would be very hard. She knew what her heart told her, she wanted to be with her husband wherever he was going to be, and her mind was made up. They packed their few belongings into two small suitcases including Jean's rag doll. "I can carry my teddy bear with me." Jean said.

"No, you can't," her Mum said, "you are too old at seven to be carrying a teddy bear around and there won't be any room in our cabin as we'll be sharing with two other ladies." Jean felt tears spilling down her cheeks, but she knew that she had to be grown up about it, after all they were going to see her father and she didn't want him to think she was being a baby.

Three weeks later Florence and Jean held hands as the ship started to dock in Mombasa's harbor. Peering through the rails Jean jumped up and down with excitement. "Mummy can you see him is he there?"

Florence studied the group standing on the quay as they got closer and then suddenly, she saw him.

"Oh Jean, your Daddy is right there waiting for us just as he promised to be." Her heart overflowed with relief and thankfulness. They had arrived safely and their new life together was about to begin. Embarking, they flew into Ron's arms hugging each other. He picked up their two small suitcases and put them in a car to take them to the railway station. There they boarded the train for the long three day journey from Kenya to Kampala in Uganda.

Africa - a new world and one that would share its mysteries, its joys, and its heartbreaks for many years to come.

CHAPTER 3

The train chugged along leaving a black smoky trail behind it. Jean's excitement grew by the minute looking out of the window, it was so beautiful. Vast areas of green land stretching as far as the eye could see. The route was dotted here and there with thatched mud huts and people who were black would wave and smile at them as they passed by. Sometimes animals that she had only seen pictures of in her books would appear. She saw zebras, elephants, giraffes, and even some lions and antelope. Her eyes grew wider as she took in these new sights...

what a difference from the sad and broken buildings and hearts they had left behind in England.

The train pulled into a station and chattering women wearing brightly colored clothes speaking in a different language ran up and down the platform trying to sell their goods. Bananas, papaya, sugar cane, and wooden carved animals were all being held up at windows for them to buy. Her father said, "The train stays here for 30 minutes so let's get out and stretch our legs." They stepped down and were immediately surrounded by a jostling crowd pushing into them determined to make a sale. He quickly bought some fruit and a carving each for Florence and Jean and they hopped back on the train. The experience was a little frightening for them in this new and strange country. The trains' whistle sounded loud and clear as they left the station behind and headed for their final destination and new home in Uganda.

A driver was waiting to pick them up when they arrived in Kampala and a long red murram road led from the train station. It passed through jungle interspersed and by occasional small huts and Africans carrying large bundles of firewood as well as women with babies strapped to their backs. Before long they turned into a driveway leading to a small white house surrounded by trees and colorful white and red frangipani trees, agapanthas, and red-yellow brilliant oleanders all grew in profusion. A grassy lawn surrounded the house; it looked picture perfect.

They were greeted by two Africans with big smiles on their faces., "Jambo Bwana, Memsahib and memsahib kidogo …we welcome you to your new home," they said. Florence and Jean were overcome with amazement. It was all so very different to everything they had ever known. They had arrived, this was the beginning of their new life in Africa.

"It will take you a while to get used to the way of life here," Ron said. "The servants were greeting you in their language called Swahili. They understand some English, but you may have to show them what you need doing. We have no electricity and have to use paraffin lamps in the evening for lighting. Our water supply comes from a water tank on the roof which fills up when we get the rain. Our toilets are buckets tucked behind a door in the bathroom and they get emptied for us every day." Florence held her breath after all this was Africa, but she didn't expect it to be quite so primitive.

After exploring the rest of the house she asked where the kitchen was. "I don't think you will want to cook when you see where it is… I have hired a cook for us." He led her outside to a small hut. Smoke poured out as he opened the door revealing a wood fire stoking a primitive looking stove. The cook turned towards them with a big toothless grin on his face as he wiped his hands down a very dirty apron. A huge cockroach wriggled out of the woodwork and dropped to the floor. Jean squealed with fright as he stamped on it with his bare foot. Ron put his arm around Florence. "This will all take time to get used to, but we are fortunate to have a home of our own. I have a good job training Africans to have their own government."

Britain had governed Uganda since 1894. It was a British Protectorate during the time of the British Empire. This meant that the British would eventually help them to form their own government and it was now time for them to govern themselves. "Before we came there were many tribal wars and now they want to unite the country under their own government."

That night after Jean had been put to bed under her mosquito net, they sat under the lamplight quietly reminiscing about the difficult years they had spent apart and talking about about their future in this new country.

CHAPTER 4

Jean with Dog Toby

Jean ran in from the garden jumping up and down with excitement. "There's a snake it's so big and the gardener got a panga and chopped its head off. It kept on wriggling for ages even without its head!" She had adapted so quickly to this new way of life, Florence thought. She had made friends with the servants' children right away and ran around wildly barefoot exploring everything that they were showing her. She was fascinated by the anthills with colonies of ants running up and down, but she learned very quickly not to get too close. They had vicious bites and couldn't be shaken off easily. She tried eating their food called posho which was maize cornflour mixed to a porridge like consistency and she would eat with her fingers just like they did. She got jiggers in her feet. These were tiny insects the size of a pin-point. They would get under the skin of the feet where they laid eggs which appeared like a blister. The servants knew how to extract them without breaking the bag that enclosed their eggs. She learnt to be brave like her friends when they were being removed with a needle.

"She is getting so out of hand," Florence said to Ron. "What do you think we should do?"

"My thoughts," said Ron, "are that it is time for her to go away to school. She is 8 years old and has already missed some education because of the war." Florence nodded in agreement, but her heart sank. She knew that there were no schools in Uganda and they would have to send her to boarding school in Kenya. It would be so far away and she was still so young. It was a decision that had to be made. There was no alternative.

CHAPTER 5

J ean was excited about her new uniform and the thought of going to a big girl's school. She stood on the platform of the train station with a dozen other girls of different ages. Parents were talking to each other and one mother brought her daughter over to them. "This is my daughter's first time to go away to school and it looks like it may be the first time for your daughter too." The two girls looked at each other.

"I'm Jean. What's your name?" Jean said.

"Mine is Molly," the girl said. It was time for them to get on board the train. Jean felt a sudden jolt of panic in the pit of her stomach. She was leaving her parents and tears started to well up in her eyes. Molly reached out her hand and yanked her towards the train. "Don't cry otherwise you will be labeled a cry baby and they will tease you. My sister told me this and she is one of the senior girls." Jean gulped back her tears as she kissed her parents goodbye.

The train pulled slowly out of the station as she waved at her parents through the window until they were out of sight. The girls sat in the compartment with an escort who told them what would be happening during the two days and one night on the train until they reached their school. Jean and Molly soon became fast friends, a friendship that sustained them through many new and sometimes frightening experiences that they would face in the years ahead.

CHAPTER 6

The train rocked and screeched as the brakes brought it slowly to halt. "Pick up your bags and follow me," the escort said. "Stay in line and no talking." They were hustled into a rickety bus as they shivered in the early morning light. The road was very windy and bumpy as they traveled towards their new school. Out of the shadows dark forbidding buildings appeared. The escorts voice came over a loudspeaker, "Stand up and move forward when I tell you to, there will be no chattering or giggling or you will face the consequences." Molly squeezed Jean's hand, they both felt the same way. They were overcome with fear and dread of the unknown. What would they do to them if they did something wrong?

They were ushered into a big empty hall where they pinned their names on their uniforms and were given a mug of hot chocolate. The Principal and some teachers placed them in groups and they were separated from each other. Jean started to cry and was immediately taken to one side by an angry looking woman, "Stop this right at once otherwise you will be punished. We don't want you to make everyone else start crying," she said as she pulled her roughly back into one of the groups. Jean hung her head in shame as the others all stared at her. They were all marched off to their dorms allocated a bed and a locker. Molly persuaded one of the other girls to swop beds so she could be next to Jean. At least they could whisper to each other at night when the lights were turned off. They were both feeling so alone and missing their families.

They gradually learned how to cope in this new constricted world of boarding school full of strict rules and constant discipline. Their days started with Assembly in the large hall. The Principal came in and said, "Good morning " to which they all respond dutifully "Good morning, Ma'am." A prayer was said followed by a hymn and then they all scurried off to their classrooms. Meals were served on long tables and after grace they could sit down and eat, but anyone with bad table manners was sent out and missed their meal. No one could leave the table until all had finished their food whether they liked it or not.

The best part of the day was the afternoon when sports were played. Jean loved the freedom of being able to run outside in the hockey and netball games. If they disobeyed any of the rules they were disciplined with a cane hitting hard on their hands 5 times. At night if caught talking they were made to sit outside on a cold hard floor for several hours at a time. Both girls got into trouble several times as it was so hard to live under such strict rules. They whispered quietly about running away, but where could they run to they were so far from home.

CHAPTER 7

One day at Assembly a man was introduced to the school. He was a Pastor from a church nearby. "We are opening a program for 8 year olds to come for two hours on Sundays, called Crusaders, and some of you will be chosen to come." Jean and Molly jumped at the idea anything to get out of this horrible place. They tried to be on their best behavior but they were chosen anyway because the teachers thought they needed to be taught how to repent!

The following Sunday, 10 of them went excitedly to Church. The service was boring but afterwards they took them to a room where there was a table laden with sandwiches and cakes. "Help yourselves girls," said some kind ladies who handed them plates. "There is lemonade over in the jug."

Jean caught Molly's eye "This must be the heaven they talked about in the church," she said. They both giggled and went to fill up their plates. After tea they had something called a Bible Study where they talked about God and His son Jesus. It sounded terrible... God had allowed his son to be crucified. What a terrible Father he must be surely this wasn't the same heavenly Father she had heard of a long time ago. He was supposed to be kind and loving and her Grandma was with Him. She felt very confused about all of this.

On the way home Molly asked her if she would go again next week. "Don't think so," she said, but then the memory of all the delicious cakes popped into her mind, "Oh I 'll maybe give it another try the people were so nice." she said.

Jean knelt on the small pillow against the pew on the church floor as prayers were being chanted. Peeking through her folded fingers she gazed up at the altar while the priest droned on. The large cross caught her eye and sun light from the stained-glass windows cast rainbow colors over it appearing to make it shimmer. It was so beautiful she couldn't imagine why they had used it to hang Jesus on, and what did they use to hang him with. Everyone started to get up and sit on their seats and a man walked out in front of the altar.

"I have come to visit the church today," he said. "I am a missionary from America and I have come to tell you the good news about Jesus." He started telling the story of Jesus's birth to a young virgin and His birth in a stable. How He grew to be a man and did many, good miracles like healing the blind and the lame. He had friends called disciples and He said that He was the son of God who had come to save mankind from their sins. He claimed that God would forgive their sins if they turned to Him and asked for forgiveness and mend their ways. The ruling priests at this time did not believe Him and turned him over to the Romans who crucified Him. The Romans governed the country at that time and He was beaten and they put a crown of thorns on His head and nailed Him to a cross. Jesus had told his disciples that when he died he would rise up again in three days and that was what happened. 500 people saw Him and talked with Him after He had died and was put in a grave. He said that if we believe and put our faith in Him we will also be made alive again after we die and will be with Him in heaven.

Jean thought about her Grandma... maybe Jesus had brought her back to life again. The man paused and then asked them to bow their heads. "If you want to be saved by Jesus just ask him to come into your heart; He will save you!" he said. "Stand up and come to the altar." His voice changed and became loud and threatening, "If you don't come to him you will go to Hades! The end of the world is coming soon and you will burn forever in Hades!" Jean felt a shiver of terror run down her back....what was going on? She was suddenly feeling very scared.

Molly grabbed her hand, "C'mon, we had better go." They walked up to the man hand in hand with several others and stood wondering what would happen next. Walking over to them he put a hand on each of their heads.

"Do you want to be saved?" he asked.

"Yes, yes" they both blurted out. Hades wasn't a place they wanted to go it was a terrifying thought. They were each given a bible and the service came to an end after a final blessing by the priest.

Neither of them said a word on the way back to school but both were trying to make sense of what had happened. In the years that followed the memory of this faded and as both girls eventually moved on to new schools they left those memories behind or so they thought.

CHAPTER 8

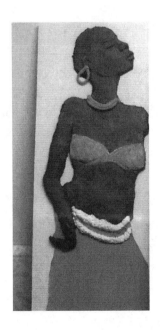

The days passed too slowly as it came near to the end of term. Jean crossed each day off on a calendar as she couldn't wait to go home and see her parents again. She had moved to a new school when she turned twelve years old. She had grown used to being in boarding school and had lots of friends, but she always missed her parents and couldn't wait to go home. She was looking forward to seeing her baby brother, David, who was now two years old. Her parents had moved to a town near Lake Victoria. In her mother's weekly letter she described how pretty it was and how they were able to swim in the lake. They had a new dog, some chickens, and ducks... she couldn't wait. At last the day arrived and they were back on the train again. At last she was on her way home.

Her parents were waiting on the platform as the train pulled into the station. She flung herself into their arms as she got off the train and talked nonstop until arriving at their new home. Toby, their new dog, ran out to the car barking and the moment she opened the door he bounded onto her lap licking her face with wet doggie kisses. It was love at first sight. David broke free from his Ayah's hand and wrapped himself around her legs as she got out of the car. From that moment on they were both at her heels wherever she went. They now had chickens and ducks and David's special pets, a one eyed pigeon called Nelson who strutted around keeping them all in order. There was a Guinea Fowl with one leg that had miraculously survived being shot and rescued by David as a pet instead of being sentenced to death for the dinner table. Everything was so much better. They now had electricity, running water, and a calor gas stove for her mother who could now bake everything from home made fresh bread to delicious dinners. Africans would come to the door selling fish from the lake and fresh fruit and vegetables. After stodgy school food it all tasted so good.

She loved the Ugandan people too. They were so different from the Kenyans who were unfriendly and sometimes quite surly. Even though the people in Uganda did not have much money they were happy, quick to smile, and laugh a lot. They loved music and dancing their tribal dances. Their village was several miles away and sometimes the sound of their drums and the rhythm of the music would resonate through the night air. She wanted to go and join them. She gradually learned their language and was able to barter in the market place with the local people.

One day when she was there with the house servants and the normal chatter suddenly stopped and people went very quiet.

"What is happening?" she asked the woman selling vegetables.

"It is the Witch Doctor," she said "he is coming here." Jean heard a wailing as a man dressed in animal skins. He had the black and white skin of a colobus monkey around his chest and a leopard skin draped over his shoulder. His headdress was the pelt of a red monkey. He carried cow bells which he rattled as he walked into the center place of the market. He was a frightening sight and it was as if an invisible thread pulled everyone into a circle around him. His voice grew loud and he pointed to someone in the crowd. A woman moved toward him and knelt on the ground in front of him. He raised his stick over her chanting something. She screamed as her body started to thrash around violently. It was a terrifying sight and Jean shrank back. Finally the woman lay prostate on the ground. No one moved toward her. The Witch Doctor turned and walked away and everyone started to go back to their stall talking again and taking no notice of the woman who still lay twitching on the ground. Was she still alive? What had happened?

Jean turned her gaze to the stall holder who was back trying to sell vegetables again. "What happened to that poor woman "she asked.

"Oh, he was the Witchdoctor who both heals or condemns. That person was condemned and he put a spell on her. Her husband had accused her of being unfaithful so he called him to punish her. If the accusation wasn't true she would have been given a healing and not suffered. The Witchdoctor has supernatural powers to heal or to make her ill or die." Jean looked over at the woman who had been struck down. She was struggling to get on her feet.

"Can't anyone help her?" she asked.

"No," the woman said "we must not touch her because it would be bad luck for us. "She will live or die according to what the Witchdoctor has decided." Jean turned away tears filling her eyes. This was so cruel and unfair but it was a belief that these people had and she had no answer to it.

This was the Africa that she had come to love, but there were dark secrets that she was only beginning to find out.

CHAPTER 9

Toby ran across the lawn chasing the ducks who took to the air honking in annoyance. They circled around above her and headed off for the safety of the lake. The sky was a brilliant blue color broken up with fluffy white clouds floating slowly across causing shadows to fall over the lake. She squinted her eyes. What was she seeing? Was her imagination playing tricks on her? A grey column was coming down from the sky to the lake. It grew fast getting wider and bigger until it reached the lake. This was weird and scary. She shut her eyes and opened them again. It was still there.

A feeling of panic started to rise up in her chest and memories of her earlier childhood teaching about the end of the world came flooding into her mind. She remembered the Preacher who had warned Molly and her that strange signs and wonders would appear in the sky before Jesus came down to judge everyone on earth. Was Jesus coming and would he send her to Hades? No one had helped her to understand the bible so she had stopped trying to read it a long time ago. It didn't seem to make any sense.

Jean's heart was pounding as she ran towards the house. Her mother was in the kitchen as she fell in through the door. "Mum you have to come outside there is something so scary appearing over the lake."

Her mother looked up, "What is it Jean?" her mother said. She realized that she was frightened so she stepped outside quickly and looked towards the lake. Putting her arm around her daughter she said "Oh Jean, you don't need to worry it is a waterspout. These come from condensation in the clouds which funnel down into the water like a tornado. They can move over the water for a while but they don't do as much damage as a tornado and gradually disappear. Jean let out a sigh of relief. She didn't tell her mother about her fears. Her parents did not go to church and they might not understand.

CHAPTER 10

R on decided to take both of them with him on one of his many
journeys to tea, coffee, and sugar plantations. Part of his job was
to ensure that they were being run properly and that the labor forces
were being treated well. He worked with the Labor Department of the
government and it was important to install good working conditions
and relationships in Uganda before the British handed it over to the
fledgling African government. Uganda was a Protectorate and would
become self-governing once Africans were able to take over.

They set off in the cool of the early morning for their long journey
south west with their final destination being the Ruwenzori Mountains,
also known as the Mountains of the Moon. These were on the eastern
side of the great African Rift Valley. The forest there was supposed
to have gorillas as well as pygmies, who were very tiny people living
there. They were going to make several stops at plantations on the way
where Ron could evaluate how they were doing. Jean sat in the back of
the truck as they bumped along over red murram roads sending dust
billowing out behind them. It was like being in a dust storm when they
met occasional traffic going the other way.

At lunch time Ron pulled over to the side of the road where there
was a shady tree. They all got out and Florence brought out a blanket to
sit on and a picnic basket she had prepared for them. It was a welcome
break and they enjoyed the tasty sandwiches and fruit. It was time to
pack up and get back on the road again, but not before they "went to
see Africa." This was a phrase used by all who lived there which meant

they were going behind the bushes to go to the bathroom. There were no rest stops with toilets in Africa. Florence and Jean headed for the nearest bushes knowing that it wasn't safe to go far from the truck.

They both let out a scream at the same time. Ron came running back, "What's happening?" he shouted as he tore into the bush. He knew immediately as huge safari fire ants swarmed up his legs. They were all frantically trying to brush them off but they clung tightly biting fiercely. "Get out! Run to the truck!" They all rushed out with ants moving rapidly up into their bodies. They had walked into safari ants that were on the move. These army ants were renowned for moving in wide swathes stretching for miles and would eat everything in their path including mammals. Even small babies had been eaten. They were deterred by nothing and when they came to water the ants in front would roll into a ball and make a bridge for their army to crossover. Ron grabbed the spare gasoline tank from the truck and poured some on the blanket wiping it over the ants which started to drop off. Water would have done nothing.

On the road they were out of the direction that the ants were moving so they felt safe and relieved to get back in the truck. Their first stop was at an Indian plantation. Jean's father told them that there were many Indians in Uganda and that the British had originally brought them there over 100 years ago to work as labourers on a railway. They were very industrious people and now owned many plantations as well as shops called dukas. They were greeted warmly. Ron did a tour of the property, checked their books, and spoke with some of the Ugandan workers while the ladies took Florence and Jean to see their lovely home. The women wore the most beautiful saris and walked with such grace. In the evening they were treated to a delicious spicy Indian dinner before they left to go to a nearby Government rest home where they could spend the night.

It would take them several days to get to Fort Portal. This was the town they would stay in while they went to explore the mountains. Jean was looking forward to seeing the Mountains of the Moon; they sounded so mysterious. Her father explained that a Greek explorer called Diogenes had given them this name many centuries earlier because of their white mountain tops. When the moon rose over their peaks it was a mystical sight… almost as if the moon was giving birth to the mountains. He also believed that they held the secret of the source of the great river Nile. However, it wasn't until 1858 that an English explorer called John Speke discovered that the source came from Lake Victoria, the very lake that was so close to their home.

They arrived late afternoon and checked into their small hotel and were all so glad to have showers to wash off the dust of a very long and hot journey. Dinner was served outside on the veranda where they could enjoy a view of the mountains as the sun went down. The sky turned into brilliant colors of orange, red, and gold in the setting sun gradually changing into the deep black velvet of an African night. Millions of stars flooded the night sky showing pinpoints of light as far as the eye could see. The chirping of crickets built up around them as birds settled down for the night and occasional barking of monkeys and other creatures of the forest broke the silence as they looked towards the mountains. Out of the darkness an enormous red blood moon rose slowly over the snowcapped peaks casting a luminous glow over the mountains and the forest below it was a magical sight and they could understand how so many ancient myths and stories had taken root in these mysterious mountains. The sudden sound of African drums beating rhythmically seemed to resonate through the night air stirring something deep and primeval in Jean. She felt a sense of being part of the music as her heart beat faster attuned to the rhythm of the drums. It was both exhilarating and yet frightening. This was Africa and she knew that it would always hold a special place in her heart.

CHAPTER 11

Hiking into the rainforest the next day they struggled along a trail through thick undergrowth. Overhanging branches from the trees seemed to press in on them and the tropical heat felt suffocating. Both Florence and Jean felt nervous, it was creepy. The snap of a branch made them jump - were these the strange people they had heard about watching them.

"Can we go back?" Jean said, "I feel scared."

"We'll just go a little bit further," Ron said. Just then a tiny figure appeared in front of them wielding a spear and wearing nothing but a loincloth made of bark. They all froze.

"Stand still and don't speak..." Ron said under his breath. He held out his hands palms upward hoping that they would understand that they meant no harm and carried no weapons. The little man beckoned toward the trees making a strange grunting sound and silently some women and children started to emerge and the women were even smaller than the little man standing only about three feet tall. Apart from a string of beads around their necks they were bare breasted and wearing a similar loincloth to the men. Children looking like little dolls were clinging to their breasts or hiding behind their legs. Florence and Jean stared in utter shock and amazement. Were these the fabled pygmies who originated from the first hunter gatherers known to man?

They didn't appear to be threatening and chattered to their Chief who suddenly sent them back into the dense trees. Turning towards

Ron he pointed his spear towards him making it obvious that he wanted them to follow him.

"We'd better go," Ron said, "although he is small I'm sure he is really accurate with that spear and it may be tipped with poison." Florence and Jean clung together too frightened to do anything other than just follow along. Several yards in they came to a clearing which appeared to be a small village surrounded by mud huts. A fire was burning in the center of a circle and as they approached the sound of drums started as the villagers all gathered around. A woman came and took their hands and led them to a place on the ground to sit. Once again the rhythmic beat of the drums raised their already heightened senses. A wooden bowl was passed around and they were urged to drink. It was a foul-tasting liquid, but fortunately they only had a small sip as the bowl was so tiny. They began to feel ethereal and very relaxed. The drums slowly went silent as a Witch doctor stepped into the middle of the circle. He was much smaller, but similar to the Witch doctor that Jean remembered from the marketplace. He sat down opening his bag spilling the contents of bones, feathers, and his shaman herbal remedies onto the ground. Arranging the bones as they fell he then moved around the circle chanting incantations over each person until he came to them. He waved feathers over them shouting in a loud and aggressive way and pointing a bony finger at each of them he made some grunting noises.

They stayed completely silent as they sensed a cloud of darkness swirling around them.

He suddenly stopped pointing at them and held out his hand, "He wants us to give him something," Ron muttered quietly under his breath. "Give him your bracelet, Florence, and anything you have in your pocket, Jean." Ron gave him some money as Florence slipped off her bracelet and handed it to him. Jean dug through her pocket and found a Saint Christopher medallion that she carried round with her. A friend had given this to her to take with her whenever she traveled. Saint Christopher was the patron Saint of travelers and supposed to keep her safe. Reluctantly she handed it over to this frightening little man. He grabbed it and then let out a howling scream and flung it on the ground. Stepping backwards he turned and ran. Jean picked it up as all the people turned away and melted into the forest and they were left on their own.

"Let's get out of here fast," said Ron as they stumbled through the brush and back onto the trail. None of them spoke until they got back into the truck. It seemed like a bad dream.

"Do you think that God kept us safe?" Florence said. "It does seem as if there were supernatural powers at work. That Witch doctor was an evil man and certainly felt the power of goodness when he took the medallion in his hand. There is so much we don't understand." Jean nodded, but once again she went back to all the questions she still had after her church experience at school so many years ago.

CHAPTER 12

"One more stop on the way home," Ron said. "We will go to visit Jack, Beetle, and Spadge at their camp in Namaherere. Jeans spirit lifted she always loved to visit these people who were like family to them. The two brothers and sister Spadge had moved to Africa many years ago with their mother who had now passed away. They were mining for Tungsten which was a metal alloy used to strengthen steel. Their camp was out in the bush and had a central building and three rondavels with thatched roofs which were equipped to house guests. Toilets were outside in a hut which had a long deep earth hole. It was always scary to visit as there was no telling what you might find in there, including the occasional snake.

They were self-sufficient growing their own food and had dogs, chickens, ducks, and rabbits and they shot deer for meat. They had two tame crested crane birds called Herbert and Harriet who always turned up at the breakfast table to claim their treats. Jean felt very spoilt when she was there and this time they said she was old enough to learn to shoot. Keeping to their word they put a gun in her hand and pointed her towards tin can targets which she mastered very quickly. She felt very grown up, but didn't feel that she would ever be able to shoot an animal.

That night over dinner there was talk of a leopard sighting nearby. The dogs started barking and one of the servants ran in, "Come quickly, Bwana we have seen the leopard it's in a tree right outside the door." Jack and Beetle grabbed their guns and ran outside as this was a real danger to the workers at the camp. The dogs were going wild as the leopard was making its way down the tree and suddenly it leaped straight at one of the workers who was watching in the shadows. He went down with an agonizing scream as the dogs ran over and Beetle leveled his gun directly at the creature mauling this poor man. The dogs were darting in and out of the fray which was making it hard to get a clear shot. Momentarily distracted, the leopard turned on the dogs and he took aim and shot. Yelping and squealing one dog was in the leopard's mouth. In quick succession he fired two shots killing the leopard and the dog.

The badly injured man was surrounded by a group of people as Spadge tried to stem the bleeding and giving orders to bring the truck around to take him to the nearest hospital several miles away.

"Will he be alright?" Jean asked.

"No telling," Spadge said, "he was very badly injured." They all went back inside and opened a bottle of whiskey passing a glass to each of them. Jean was allowed a little sip and she suddenly started to feel more relaxed and calmer after the horrible sight she had just witnessed. The leopard was such a beautiful creature and yet so wild and savage just like the Africa she had grown to know and love so well.

CHAPTER 13

They packed up the next morning and started off for home. Jean was not looking forward to it after their exciting trip and it was nearly time to go back to school.

The long, dusty bumpy road seemed endless and it was a welcome relief to have a raucous welcome from her brother David and Toby who wildly ran round in circles barking wildly. Her little brother seemed to have grown again even in the short time they had been away. He held her hand tightly pulling her over to see his pets again. His one-legged Guinea Fowl had disappeared and nobody seemed to know how it got away.

That night young David was allowed to stay up late for dinner with them all. A large roast chicken surrounded by roasted potatoes was brought in from the kitchen which looked delicious. They were all starving and ready to eat when a howl of anguish came from David.

"That's my Guinea fowl!" he cried out.

"Nonsense, it's just a chicken," said Ron.

"No, look at it…look…it only has one leg," David said crying. They all looked.

"Well….the other leg must have fallen off in the kitchen," Ron said. They all went quiet as David ran out sobbing. Florence went out to comfort him, but and a tinge of guilt set in as they realized they were about to eat his beloved pet.

CHAPTER 14

The summer months rolled on and Jean knew that she was going to high school in Nairobi in the autumn. She wasn't sure how many of her friends would be going there. Friends were so important when you were so far from home. It would be a big transition from Junior school. She knew that some of the girls came from farming families in Kenya so they would probably be there but some of the girls from Uganda may be going to other schools. The school had six hundred white girls. She had hoped some boys would be there, but it seemed that boys were sent to all boys' schools. It seemed to her that whoever was planning these schools were determined not to let them get distracted or have any fun.

The days flew by as her mother organized her new school uniform and sewed her name onto everything. Paperwork was completed and she was once again on her way to the station. She felt nervous and not just because she was going to a new school. She had heard her parents talking after she had gone to bed. Her father had said that there was a talk of an uprising in Kenya. It was about the Africans wanting self-government and getting rid of the British. He felt it was just a rumor and said they had good security forces there so he didn't think that there would be a problem.

"Do you think Jean will be alright?" Florence asked, "will she be safe?"

"I wouldn't let her go if I didn't feel secure about it," he said. "There is no school here for her to go to and she needs to have a good education. We will let her go."

The school appeared to be so much larger than her previous elementary and Junior schools. A bus picked them up from the railway station to take them many miles to the school. The school was in the suburbs of the large sprawling town called Nairobi. Enormous iron gates opened up as they approached, and then they were waved in by two African Askaris security guards. A high barbed wire fence surrounded the property and some tall brick towers appeared to surround the buildings inside. Four large two story buildings stood in a semi-circle with grass, connecting them to other buildings which turned out to be the main assembly hall, classrooms, and dining room.

Girls were being off loaded from buses at their various buildings. Each was named after a famous person, and Jean was assigned to the Huxley house named after Elspeth Huxley. She was a well-known author who was a pioneer in Kenya and had arrived in Kenya with her family in 1912. They were taken upstairs to their dormitories and Jean was thrilled to see Molly, Alli, and two of her other friends from junior school already unpacking their bags. They all jumped up and down with excitement hugging each other until the stern voice of the Housemistress said "Stop this silliness right away, finish your unpacking immediately, and follow me." They knew right then that she would come down hard on them if they didn't obey the rules.

They headed towards the dining room and sat at tables of ten for meals and sang grace before eating. Food was placed in front of them and they had to eat everything on their plate whether they liked it or not. No one was allowed to leave until everyone had finished. Jean realized how hard that was when one day a small caterpillar crawled out from under her lettuce. She refused to eat the lettuce and had to sit there with nine stony faced girls who wanted to leave. She finally gave in and promptly threw up for which she had further punishments. Once again she found herself struggling against ridiculous rules that fought against her free spirit.

She settled down eventually and did her best to conform, but somehow she and her friends seemed to get into trouble. Six of them came close to being expelled when they were caught trying to smoke in the closets at the end of the dorm. They thought they were hidden inside the closets but the smoke gave them away and they were dragged out coughing and feeling sick. They were made to stand in front of the whole school of six hundred girls at Assembly the next morning where they were disgraced and sent to the Principal's office. They were put on probation and told that they would be expelled if there were any more misdemeanors, and would be given a punishment that would make them think twice before doing anything like that again.

The time came for her and other girls whose families were from the Church of England to be confirmed. They went to Confirmation classes which gave Jean more of an understanding of what the Christian faith was about. Once more she was hearing about the birth, death, and resurrection of Jesus. The same story she had heard when she had gone to Crusaders bible meeting when she was so young. Although she understood more now and believed that God was good she questioned the teaching that Jesus was the only way to God and that if you did not believe you would go to hell. Surely, this was not what Jesus would do after all His miracles, His love, and going to the cross voluntarily to take our sins away and make us acceptable to God. What about the people who were good and believed in another way to God or if they came from a different religion or had never heard of Jesus? However, she decided to go ahead with it and be able to take Communion. Besides she thought, I get to wear a pretty white dress and a white veil, it would be looking like a bride and that was very appealing.

CHAPTER 15

Things seemed to be going better by the time she went back for the next year at school. She was working harder at her studies, had a great group of friends, and they were allowed a little more freedom. They even arranged for a dance to be held with a neighboring boys' school. This was the most exciting thing that had happened and they all talked about nothing else other than what they would wear and if they might get a boyfriend. The dance was scheduled to be held in the Assembly Hall.

The girls were waiting as the boys bus drove up and they all came in. Most of them looked so embarrassed and as the music started they began to look like rabbits in the headlights and were making no moves to ask the girls to dance. Jean and her friends decided to put them out of their misery and went over to ask them instead. Jean's potential victim refused to get up and dance so she sat down beside him and asked him his name.

"Nick," he said and she asked him if he came from Uganda or Kenya. "My family has a farm in Kenya, but I have to go to boarding school because we live so far away and it is out in the bush."

"Oh that must be so nice to live on a farm. I always thought I'd like to live on a farm, it must be so much fun," said Jean.

"Not so. It is really hard work and almost a relief to go to school, especially now."

"What do you mean?" Jean asked.

"Well you probably don't know much about it, but things are not very safe right now there is an uprising by the Kikuyu Africans who want independence from the British and they want to take our farms for themselves. Our farm has been in the family for three generations. They have a group of terrorists called the Mau Mau who force people to join them… making them go through terrible unspeakable rituals, and they are attacking some of the farms. They are killing people and maiming animals in the most brutal way."

Jean swallowed hard. This was dreadful. She had not heard of anything about this and she found herself reaching out for his hand, "I am so sorry. You must be so worried for your family," she said.

To her surprise he grasped her hand and held it tightly, "Yes I am, but my father has guns and dogs as well as security men from another tribe so I hope they will be safe." He stood up and pulled her to her feet and said, "let's dance!" They joined the others who had now lost all their inhibitions and were dancing wildly on the floor. When they left later that evening he scribbled his address on some paper and thrust it in her hand. "Write to me. I'd really like to keep in touch."

Jean's thoughts went back to the night before she had left home. Was this what her father had been talking about - an uprising? She thought about the barbed wire fence she saw when coming into the school through the huge iron gate, and started thinking about floodlights that had been installed recently in the towers around the school. Were they afraid that they might be attacked? Thoughts spun around her head.

"So…." her friend Alli said, "what was going on with you and that boy. You both looked so serious….was he asking you to be his girlfriend?"

"Of course not. He was just telling me about his family." She did not want to pass anything on to her about what she had heard, because she knew that Alli came from a farming family and she didn't want to frighten her.

A few nights after the dance the floodlights in the towers were turned on at night, lighting the area all around the fence. An announcement was made during Assembly to say that there had been some robberies in the area and this was for taking precautions. Rumors started going around about murders on some of the outlying farms. They heard that a white farmer, his wife, and the Kikuyu people who worked for them had all been brutally hacked to death by machetes. They were all really shocked and scared - could this really be true?

CHAPTER 16

A visit to an Agricultural Farming Show had been scheduled which the girls thought may be cancelled, but when they heard they would still be going to it they felt relieved and confident it must be safe and maybe the rumors were just rumors. The buses picked up the girls who were allowed to go and dropped them off at the entrance to the farm show where they handed over their tickets.

The younger girls had to go round in groups with an escort, but the older girls could walk around on their own. All of them would regroup at the gate by 4:00 p.m. Jean and her five friends started off towards the food tent where they picked up something to eat and fizzy Fanta orange drinks. This was going to be so much fun and there was a lot to see. They headed for the flower, fruit, and vegetable tent and decided to split up and at that point. Then Jean and Molly walked over to see the animals. They were fascinated by the auctioneers bidding over some Jersey milk cows. Turning around to leave they bumped into three young soldiers in Khaki uniforms. They all laughed and introduced themselves.

"You young girls shouldn't be walking around here on your own," said Harold who seemed to be in charge. "We will walk round with you if you like." The girls jumped at the idea, who wouldn't want to be escorted by three good looking military guys. It was a lot of fun and they ended up at the food tent again for coffee.

Before they left Jean and Molly asked them about their jobs. "What do you do in the military?"

"We are fighting against the Mau Mau uprising," said Mike as he glanced over at Harold. "Should we tell them what goes on?"

"Definitely not!" said Harold. "We should not be telling them horror stories."

"We just go into the forest of the Aberdare mountains to track down the Mau Mau who are terrorists and who are killing a lot of people, both black and white."

Mike jumped in, "We have to blacken our faces and we find where they initiate people with their gruesome ceremonies and ...."

"Stop right now!" Harold shouted. "You will frighten these girls to death." Turning to them he said, "you have no need to worry. We are winning the war and keeping you all safe." He handed Molly a card and said that if they ever ran into trouble they could contact them. As they left Molly said to Jean "I'm going to contact him anyway. I think he is really cute!"

The Principal finally told them during Assembly one morning that there was an emergency and an uprising was taking place. She said that Jomo Kenyatta who had started the movement to remove the British from power and have self-government had been imprisoned. While he had been in jail the movement had become more violent and the Mau Mau terrorists had evolved. Things got out of hand despite the armies efforts to control it. New safety measures would be put in place at the school. No more visits outside the school including those for girls who lived nearer to the school and could occasionally be allowed to visit family. There would be soldiers seen on the campus. A siren would be sounded if there was an attack, and they would be given instructions about where they should go. If it was at night the girls should get out of bed onto the floor and pull their mattresses over the top of them. Everyone was very quiet as they left to go to their classrooms, but an insidious sense of fear seemed to settle in their minds. This was no longer rumors, but was actually real and possibly moving right into their school.

Stories that circulated around the school were became more lurid and terrifying. These terrorists were raping women and would slit open the stomachs of pregnant women and kill them and their babies. They would cut the back legs off cows and leave them to die and would nail dogs and cats to fences. There were unspeakable horrors of what would be done to them if they got into the school. Jean felt shivers run down her spine. She remembered the horrible stories her mother had told her about the war she was born into in England, and how the Jews were all taken to concentration camps where they were tortured, overworked to death, or murdered in gas ovens. This was all pure evil. Where was God when all this evil was happening....was He really there?

CHAPTER 17

Their final exams were coming up soon and they all tried to concentrate on their studies. It was only a few weeks now before the end of term when they could go home and feel safe.

Late one afternoon during study time an announcement was made over the loudspeaker. "All girls who come from Uganda need to go back to their dorms immediately." Several from Jean's class got up and they walked together wondering what all this was about. They were met by their Housemistress who told them to pack their clothes and books in their suitcases which had been put out on their beds. They felt bemused by it all until she told them that they would be going home on a train that would be leaving that evening. The school was being evacuated because in a few days Jomo Kenyatta was going to be released from prison and they were expecting riots on the streets and they did not know what would happen. They needed to keep them all safe.

They were loaded onto buses and escorted by the military to the station and put on a train. It all happened so quickly they had no time to even ask any questions. Some of the fully armed soldiers took them on board to their compartments taking down their names and telling them to stay put and keep their heads down. The train lurched out of the station on the now familiar trip back to Uganda.

Two days and nights on the train, but this time it was different. They had covered the windows and told them to be very quiet. Sandwiches and drinks were handed out and the soldiers walked up and down the corridors as they came through one of the Townships known to be a center of the terrorists. The door to their compartment slid open and a man's voice said, "I am one of the soldiers and I will be sitting with you for the next part of the journey." As they passed into a tunnel the girls were so scared that they may be attacked or blown up, but they came out safely at the other end.

The covers over the windows were removed soon after that and to their surprise, Harold who they had met at the Agricultural Show, was sitting next to them. Jean saw him snatch his hand quickly away from Molly's hand. She looked at Molly and raised eyebrows. There was obviously something going on here between them. They all cheered when Tororo Rock came into sight. This was a huge tall rock beside the railway line defining their entry point into Uganda. At last they were back on home ground and safe and sound. Molly's parents were waiting on the platform and Harold got off the train first and helped Molly to step down. Turning back to the rest of them he said, "This is where I get off I have to report back to Nairobi for duty." Jean was dying to question Molly about what she had noticed, but she was already involved with her parents.

"Write to me soon Molly," she shouted as the train started off again.

CHAPTER 18

It was so good to be home and sleep in her own bed without fear. David had been sent to boarding school in England but was home on vacation and had done some serious growing up. He was a much better companion and was no longer the little brother trailing around in her footsteps. They managed to persuade their parents to take them again to visit Spadge, Beetle, and Jack. While they were there they all went on a new adventure to meet an Italian heiress reputed to be a Countess who had bought an island in the middle of the turbulent Kagera River.

The only access to the island was by a swinging wood and rope bridge. Ron and David went over first.

"Just take a firm grip on both sides of the rope!" Ron shouted back to Florence and Jean. "Don't look down and put your feet down one after another directly in front of you. Both Florence and Jean were terrified. Below them they could see crocodiles in the water and basking on the shore.

"I'll go first Mum," said Jean as she stepped forward grasping each side of the rope bridge and putting one foot in front. The bridge rocked from side to side with each footstep and she gained confidence as she slowly moved along. Getting close to the end she glanced down, her foot slipped, and with a scream she fell. She was hanging over the edge clinging desperately to one side of the rope. One of the young African workers who was familiar with the bridge ran immediately across towards her and wound a rope around her ankles. She was still screaming with fear as he tied another rope around her body and using his strength inched her up until she was lying flat on the bridge. He told her to get up on her hands and knees and crawl the last few feet reassuring her that he had a rope around her so she couldn't fall. She collapsed on the other side in the arms of Ron and David.

Florence looked on in horror knowing full well there was no way she was going to attempt to cross over. Ron talked to the African worker who had rescued Jean thanking him for what he had done. In Swahili he asked him if he could manage to bring his wife over.

"Ndio Bwana," he said. "I can bring her by piggy back if she would be willing. She could hold fast to my back and not panic." Ron shouted instructions to Florence who was shocked but realized that it was the only way she could get across. "It's alright Memsahib," the young African said, "Just close your eyes and hold tightly around my neck and I will get you there safely." Trembling she put her arms over his strong shoulders and he hoisted her onto his back. He moved confidently across the bridge and had her there in no time.

They all followed the pathway up to the house which looked like a well-built brick building surrounded by beautiful exotic flowers and blue jacaranda trees. A grey parrot was sitting on the rail of the veranda outside the front door. "Get out…get out… get out," he squawked.

"Oh dear, this doesn't seem to be a very good welcome," said Ron. The front door opened and a slight woman dressed in a bright colored oriental caftan burst through the door.

"Hello and welcome to you all," she said with a strong Italian accent. "Come on in take no notice of my bad tempered bird." Ron introduced David and Jean to Toni as she led them inside and showed them their rooms. "If you want to shower there is an outside shower room with soap and towels…no guarantee that the water will be hot. "Cocktails will be served at 7, and dinner at 8."

They all scurried off to clean up in a makeshift wooden room. There was no roof on it but the shower seemed to work. Jean was the last one to go in and as she was scrubbing the dust off her she looked up and saw a snake wiggling its way over the wall. Grabbing the towel she started to run out. Mesmerized, she kept her eyes on it, but it appeared to be stuck just waving itself around. Something was strange it looked different than a snake… what on earth was it?" She moved forward cautiously and threw the soap at it. There was a trumpeting noise outside as the creature rapidly moved back over the wall.

After cocktails they moved into the dining room for dinner. Everyone was very talkative, the wine flowed, and there were so many stories to share. Storytelling was a big part of life in Africa.

"How was the shower?" Toni asked. "did you get hot water?"

"Yes," Jean said. "But a strange snake tried to get over the wall into the bathroom and I threw the soap at it and it disappeared."

Toni roared with laughter, "that would have been my baby elephant who was checking you out with his trunk. I have quite a few animals here that we have saved from poachers, mostly young ones whose mothers have been killed. Tomorrow I will take you round the island and you can get to meet them all." As the dinner party continued several stories were shared about close encounters with different animals. Ron made them all laugh when he recounted a story about his good friend who had been at the annual Saint Andrews dinner that was held at the golf club each year. The golf club was situated very close to Lake Victoria and in good Scottish tradition they had all drunk copious amounts of Scotch whiskey. It was dark when his friend left to get into his car to go home and he came running back a few minutes later shaking and as white as a sheet.

"What on earth happened?" Ron had asked.

"I tried to put my key in the car door and the thing just got up and walked away," he said as he collapsed on the floor. He had mistaken the dark shape for his car, and it turned out to be a hippo who was quietly grazing on the grass in front of the lake.

They were amazed to see how many animals she had collected when she took them with her the next day. There was the baby elephant, a baby rhino, two cheetah cubs, various deer, and other animals. They all wandered freely around the island. The river acted as a natural barrier so they were unable to get away.

"What happens when they get bigger?" Florence asked.

"We give them to reputable Zoos or to groups that try to rehabilitate them back into the wild. They come and take them away," replied Toni. They went out to see these beautiful animals each day and were able to help feed them. It was so good to see how well they were cared for. Happy from the trip, crossed the bridge on the way back home with much more confidence.

CHAPTER 19

There were two letters waiting for them on their arrival home. One was from the school headmistress informing them that the school was being closed indefinitely due to the unrest in Kenya. They would be sending the final Cambridge School certificate exam papers to them and Jean would be required to do the exam in a secure setting overseen by a person with legal authority. The second letter was from her friend Molly....

I know that you thought that something was up between Harold and me and you were right...... It was and I was not planning to go back to school as he has asked me to marry him. We will be taking over his father's farm near Nairobi.

Jean's heart dropped at the thought of her friend moving to a farm when farms were being attacked, but she knew that Harold would love and protect her. She also knew that her own life was going to change. Her schooldays were over and after finishing her exams she would be leaving Africa for England to pursue a career in nursing.

PART II

A New Life Ahead

CHAPTER 20

The pilot announced their approach to London Airport. "Fasten your seat belts, put your tables up, and hand any cups to the air hostesses." This was Jean's first flight on a new Britannia four engine turbo jet airliner known as the Whispering Giant, which had just come into service. She had flown as a child many years before on a BOAC Flying boat which landed on water. They had taken off from Port Bell in Uganda stopping to refuel in Khartoum, Luxor, and Cairo before landing in Southampton, England.

Her father was given leave to go back to England after three years of service in Africa, and the leave to England lasted for 3 months. This flight would take half the time and would only make 2 stops en route. She had also flown on two-engined Dakota planes which were able to land on dirt runways in Africa. That was exciting as the pilot would fly low and buzz the runway to scare off wild animals before taking off again and bringing the plane down to land.

Her thoughts were interrupted by a sudden thump as the wheels hit the runway and the plane slowed to a halt and taxied over to the passenger arrival area. They disembarked, went through immigration and customs, and walked out into the airport. It was a nerve-wracking moment…a new country and a whole new world was opening up ahead of her.

Feeling lost and alone she prayed desperately for some help. Someone tapped her on the shoulder, "Are you by any chance coming here to study nursing at Gulson Road Hospital in Coventry?" Jean felt a wave of relief sweeping over her. It seemed as if her prayer was being instantly answered and she felt so very thankful.

"I am," Jean said. "I followed your instructions to wear a red badge on my coat so I was hoping you would recognize me."

"Welcome" the woman said. "My name is Anna and I have been sent to pick you up as well as several other girls on our way back to Coventry. The drive will take us about four hours to get there and we'll stop for lunch on the way." They picked up four more girls and Anna told them what to expect when they got there. "The hospital started out in 1889 as a poor workhouse which became a hospital in 1929 mostly treating poor people. During the second world war, Coventry was decimated by the Blitz. The Germans bombed Coventry in 1940 and there were thousands of deaths and injuries. At that time Gulson Hospital opened its' doors to all casualties and made a huge contribution to the welfare of the people of the city. It is a small hospital with a big heart and we hope you will do your best to honour its tradition."

Arriving at the hospital they were welcomed inside by the Matron who was in charge of the hospital where they were joined by several other girls. Most of them seemed to be Irish, but Jean was delighted to meet a black girl who was from West Africa. They were given a quick tour of the hospital and then shown to their rooms. One of the Irish girls called Mary asked Jean to be her roommate and she jumped at the chance. The next few days were a whirl of activity as they were fitted for their uniforms, given study books, and went to lectures. It was nonstop and jet lag was out of the question.

After three months they were taken out to the wards to observe patients and were taught procedures that were used by senior nurses. They soon learned that the Staff Nurse, who was second in charge, had eyes on the back of her head and demanded perfection. At first they learned to make hospital beds, give patients bedpans, bed baths, and help feed them. Every day the top surgeon surrounded by the staff nurse and junior doctors would sweep with authority onto the various wards to visit their patients. Everything in the ward had to be perfect and patients all neatly in their beds.

One morning in the men's ward, one of the men asked for a bedpan just as the doctors were due to come in. Jean grabbed a bedpan pulled the curtains round the bed and said, "Please be as quick as you can... we are supposed to have you all sitting or lying in a perfect bed and no one behind curtains." He did his best to be quick and she hurriedly took the bedpan and started off just as the doors were flung open and in came the formidable group. Jean slipped and fell over the bedpan sliding across the floor as she heard the high pitched voice of the Staff Nurse.

"What on earth do you think you are doing, Nurse! Get up off the floor and clean it all up immediately. This is a complete disgrace! Come and see me in my office as soon as you get off duty!" Jean felt completely humiliated, but after the group left all the men cheered her and burst out laughing and said it had made their day to see the look on the faces of the very supercilious doctors.

The girls all worked hard. There were eight of them in the new group and they had fun together. The Irish girls had found a pub where you could go and sing and do Ceili dancing. The hospital had rules and you were supposed to be back in the hospital by 10:00 p.m. Jean and Mary's room was very close to the fire escape which had metal stairs leading down to the ground outside. When they went out at night they would sign out and sign back in again at 10 before climbing down the fire escape to go out for more fun. It worked really well until one night they came in late and found someone had locked the fire escape door. It was freezing outside and they huddled together on the steps leading up to the front door.

"Do you think they caught on to us?" Jean said.

"No idea." Mary said as they shivered and shook for the rest of the night.

They were both put on night shift after that for a few weeks and had to get used to staying up all night to take care of patients. One young man asked Jean if she would go on a date with him when he got out of hospital, but she turned him down. She preferred going out with Mary where they met up with a group at the Ceili dances and had so much fun. She had also kept in touch with Nick, the boy she had met at the dance in high school. They had exchanged letters occasionally and he was now in England at University. They had planned to try and meet up, but their lives had been so busy it hadn't been possible. After being at the hospital for eight months she was put on the children's wards. She was looking forward to being with children. It would be a welcome change from adults, or so she thought.

CHAPTER 21

Jean with Nurses

The children's ward was really challenging. Many of the children were really sick and needed more attention than she was able to give. "Please nurse read me a story...please nurse sit on my bed and stay with me," was often the sad tear-filled plea. Instead she had to give them injections, procedures, and pills which were so uncomfortable for them. One baby boy had hydrocephalus which was water on the brain. His head was swollen to three times the normal size and he constantly rocked his head from side to side crying out in so much pain. The parents of one young boy who was dying were asked if they would be willing to have some of his organs including his eyes harvested.

Jean couldn't cope with this, it was heartbreaking. Losing children was very difficult for her. Once again she found herself questioning

God. Why did these little ones that he was supposed to love, have to suffer so much?

One day a young mother came in with her small baby girl to the hospital. She had brought her in to see if they could find out what was wrong with her as her legs didn't appear to be working well. Jean settled her into a crib and prepared her for the doctor's examination. The mother left and never returned. She had given them a false address and they had no way of tracing her. The baby had no name and so she was named Katrina, a name chosen by Jean. The doctor diagnosed congenital hip dysplasia, a condition if not treated could cause the baby to be permanently crippled. She stayed in the hospital for a long time while they decided on the best treatment for this beautiful child, and Jean would even spend time with her after getting off duty. She bought her a soft doll, the only toy she had ever had and continued to visit her after she was transferred to another hospital for surgery. She badly wanted to adopt her, but it was impossible in her present circumstances. She was finding it just too hard to see children suffering and finally made the decision to give up her nursing career and to move on. When she handed in her resignation the Matron who was in charge of the hospital called her into the office.

"Why are you giving up after you've been here for over a year and seem to be doing so well?" she asked.

"I find it hard not to get emotionally involved with my patients," Jean said. "I really feel that I need to move on." After taking a secretarial course she took a job for a few months, but Africa was calling her back. She really missed the country she loved so much and she decided to go home.

CHAPTER 22

The plane landed in Entebbe Airport and as Jean disembarked she breathed in the familiar African smell of wood burning, and her heart lifted with joy to be back home again. A big change had taken place while she had been in England. Uganda had achieved its independence from Britain and President Milton Obote was now the leader of the Government and the country. It had been a remarkably peaceful transition and things seemed to be running well.

Her parents met her and she planned to move into an apartment with her friend Jo who had also returned recently. After just a few days she found a job. She had taken a Secretarial course in England before she left and a job had opened up as Personal Assistant to the Managing Director of East African Airways. This was ideal for her as one of the benefits of the job was that she could fly on the airline for a much reduced fare. She also managed to put a down payment on a car. Life was pretty much perfect.

Jean and Jo were welcomed back by some friends and they were both invited to a party. "This should be fun Jo, let's go. It will be great to meet up with some old friends again." They drove up to a house on Tank Hill taking a bottle of wine and anticipating a fun night out. It was great and they caught up with friends they hadn't seen in a long time and met some new people. The music and voices got louder as the drinks flowed and just before midnight they asked them all to gather in one of the other rooms. It was the night of Kenya's Independence from Britain and they said that this was going to be a special celebration.

The room quietened down in anticipation of what would happen. The partygoers started to sing derogatory songs about Kenya and then to their absolute horror they raised the British Union Jack flag. Jean and Jo looked at each other. This was shocking and beyond disrespectful.

"Let's get out of here," Jo said. "We don't want any part of this." They drove home. This was a dreadful end to a party that had started out being so much fun.

Jean got up late the next morning. It was Sunday and she loved having a lazy day. She put the kettle on for tea and popped bread into the toaster. The paper was outside the door and she put it on the table to read as she had breakfast. As she sat down it dropped onto the floor revealing the headlines and her heart started to race in panic with what she was reading.

Outrage at party on Tank Hill condemned by Government. Youth Wing demand retribution and plan to drag participants into the center of the town and have them chained up and beaten.

She shuddered and felt sick…could they really do this to them? She reached for the phone to call one of her friends who had been at the party. Her friend who picked up the phone was in hysterics, "Have you heard what happened? This has turned into a real nightmare and they are threatening to do dreadful things to us. The house on Tank Hill has been burnt down with the dogs in it. Fortunately the man that owned it was out at the time otherwise he would have been killed. They are rioting on the streets and burning some businesses. We have been told to lay low and we hope the British Embassy will step up and help us out. Luckily, for you and Jo, you were not on the party list as you were only invited at the last minute so just stay quiet and we will keep you informed about what is happening."

Returning to work the next day Jean felt that any minute a mob would suddenly appear at the door and drag her out. She was feeling very insecure and decided to ask Jo if she would like to fly down to Malindi on the coast with her for a week of vacation. They could get away from everything and try to relax on the beach. Hopefully things would settle down while they were gone. They left a few days later and soon relaxed on a beautiful white sandy beach. The crystal clear sea seemed to wash away all the frightening things that had been happening to them. Palm trees surrounded the beach and a gentle breeze lazily fluttered their fronds as they lay on the beach looking up at a vibrant blue sky where white fluffy clouds floated slowly along claiming their space in this peaceful and calm beauty. The occasional dhao bobbed along on the water and a friendly crew would wave to them. They felt all of their anxiety and fear melting away. All too soon they knew they would have to go home, and what would they find when the got there?

CHAPTER 23

The airport at Entebbe was bustling with people when they arrived and a friend was waiting to pick them up. "Stay quiet until we get out of the airport," she said. As soon as they got in the car she told them what had happened while they were gone. Apparently the Government had eventually managed to calm down the rioting mobs and had issued deportation orders for those who had organized the party. They were rounded up quickly and given 24 hours to leave the country. No one had been thrown into jail which was a huge relief to them as Ugandan jails were notorious for ill treatment of prisoners.

Life had returned to normal, but they were very wary about going to many more parties. However, Jean's friend Lizzy had just got engaged and asked her to be a bridesmaid and she was soon swept up into all the activities of helping her friend to plan her wedding. There were no shops that sold wedding or bridesmaids dresses so they all had to be made by a local Indian seamstress.

The bride looked beautiful as she walked down the aisle of All Saints Church on the day of the wedding. The train of her dress was held on each side by children, and then following were her bridesmaids. The bridegroom was in full military uniform and they made a stunning pair. As they took their vows Jean wondered if one day she might meet the man of her life and be a bride instead of a bridesmaid. When the newlyweds stepped out of the church confetti rained over them and the bride threw her bouquet into the crowd straight at her. She felt herself blushing as everyone cheered and said she would be the next bride.

The reception was held in the gardens adjoining the church where the tables were set up on the grass and vivid tropical flowers grew all around. Speeches and toasts were made and guests started to mingle as champagne flowed. The best man moved over to talk to her offering a glass of champagne. They talked for a while and he asked her if she would go on a date with him after the wedding. She agreed and they arranged to meet. However, she noticed another good-looking young man who was trying to catch her eye.

He came over and introduced himself. She felt her heart skip a beat as he asked her if she would go out with him. "Oh, I would love to," she said. "But I have already committed to go out with the Best man."

He grinned disarmingly, "Well, we could always have a date later. My name is Lawrence and I'll get in touch with you. Let me have your phone number." She wrote it down for him and as he walked away she really hoped she hadn't seen the last of him.

CHAPTER 24

Jean was invited to go on a trip to the famous Murchison Falls, one of Uganda's most beautiful treasures on the Victoria Nile with a group of friends. The Falls were situated between Lake Kyoga and Lake Albert and the waterfall fell through a narrow gap thundering down 141 feet to the river below. Jean had never seen so many wild animals on the plains as their boat travelled upstream towards the Falls. Elephants, rhino, wildebeests, zebra, and bushbuck were grazing everywhere. Crocodiles lay lazily on the banks alongside the river sunning themselves mouths wide open with white egrets picking food out of their teeth. Hippos grunted in the water and burst up to the surface at times to breathe some air. The thunderous noise of the Falls could be heard some distance away and as they approached the misty spray blew over them and the magnificent Falls came into sight.

Everyone on board gasped at the awesome beauty that they were seeing. It surely was one of God's masterpieces. A place full of wonder and myth.

Not surprising that so many visitors like members of the Royal Family, Winston Churchill, Ernest Hemingway, and so many others had made this trip. The boatman moved the boat over to the bank and asked if anyone wanted to get off and go for a short walk with a Game Warden. Jean decided to go with some of the others. None of them felt very safe as the man seemed very insecure himself even though he carried a gun. One of the men who came said, "I'm not sure that this guy knows how to use that thing and we know that there are lions around here, I think we should go back." They all agreed and headed back to the boat after all they had seen plenty of game on the way up the river. It had been a very special trip and one she would never forget.

CHAPTER 25

Lawrence the Rugby Player

Arriving home she had a call from her friend Pat asking her to come to a dinner party she was planning.

"Lawrence will pick you up," she said. "Remember him? I think you met him at the wedding."

"Yes, I'd love to come," trying not to sound too excited as her heart missed another beat. She was hoping to meet him again, but was her friend just trying to put them together or had he suggested he came to pick her up? Anyway, she really didn't know much about him except that she had found him very attractive and this would be a good time to find out.

Pat had made a very special dinner for them. She had invited two other couples and they soon started up a lively conservation after pre dinner drinks. They sat next to each other at the dinner table and kept talking until someone pointed out that that they seemed to be engrossed in their conversation.

"Well," Lawrence said, "It's the first time we've had a date so we are getting to know each other." The evening ended on a high note and as he dropped her off at home. He kissed her on the cheek and asked her if she would like to go to dinner at the best restaurant in the town the following weekend. She didn't hesitate. She already knew what her heart was telling her.

She soon learned a lot about him. He had come to Africa with a Cotton Company from Liverpool and was very ambitious about his future with the Company. He was a rugby player and golfer and took her to several of his matches. He had played rugby in three international games for Uganda against a combined Oxford Cambridge team as well as South African combined Cape Town and Stellenbosch Universities. The rugby crowd were pretty wild, but a lot of fun, and she soon fit in with the players' wives and girlfriends.

Their romance soon blossomed and they were seeing a lot of each other. Jean was in love and life was perfect.

One evening as they sat in their favourite restaurant Lawrence said, "I have something to tell you and I don't think it will make you very happy." Jean took a sip of her wine and put the glass down.

"What is it? What's happened?"

"I'm afraid I am being sent back to Head Office in Liverpool and then back to our Tanganyika office and will be leaving next week. I will write to you when I get there."

Jean's heart sank, was this going to be the end of their relationship, he hadn't suggested getting engaged or asking her not to see anyone else while he was gone. She waited for his letters which were mostly about work and when he mentioned meeting up with an old girlfriend she thought that he probably hadn't felt as committed to the relationship as she had.

The Rugby Club was holding its' annual dance and one of the wives asked her to come with them. She had a great time and one of Lawrence's best friends asked if he could take her out to another event.

She hesitated, but then agreed, after all she wasn't sure if she would even see Lawrence again. She did miss him though.

A month later his letters started to arrive regularly from Tanganyika followed by several phone calls. He had been missing her and wanted her to fly to Dar es Salaam to see him. He picked her up at the airport and took her to a friend's house where she would be staying. After dinner he said, "We will go for a swim at this lovely beach called Oyster Bay, you will love it."

The sun was setting as they arrived and the sky was a vivid kaleidoscope of orange red and yellow as it sank behind the palm trees on the fringe of the beach. They sat for a long-time holding hands in awe of the overwhelming beauty. "Let's go for a swim. The water is always warm," he said. They ran down the beach to the water and they swam as the moon rose in the sky. He wrapped his arms around her and kissed her passionately.

"I have missed you so much," he said. "Will you marry me?"

"Of course, I will!" she said as her eyes filled with tears of happiness. They sat on the beach hugging each other and talking about their future together.

"I wanted to get you an engagement ring," he said, "but there are no jeweler's shops here so why don't we meet in Nairobi in three weeks from now to buy you a ring there." As she got on the plane to fly home she felt so excited and thrilled by what had happened. She was now engaged and was going to be married, her life couldn't be more perfect.

CHAPTER 26

Lawrence drove 320 miles over dirt roads in his Ford Anglia to Nairobi stopping only once to pick up a Belgian man who was hitch hiking around Africa. It was a relief to have someone to talk to and keep him awake on the long drive. He had learned early on the dangers of falling asleep over the wheel when he had crashed at night rolling his car into a ditch on his way home from the rugby club. He had been celebrating far too well with his team mates after they had won an important match and had fallen asleep at the wheel. He had crawled out of the car and staggered up onto the road. Not a good place to be in the middle of Africa at night when he could be robbed and left for dead. He got lucky when a car finally came along and a woman got out and tried to help him. She turned out to be a doctor and cleaned the blood and dirt off and took him to the coffee estate where he lived. He was so thankful and especially as he had dropped Jean off at home so she hadn't been in the car with him, because the car had landed upside down in water in the ditch and one of them may not have made it out alive.

The Belgian was very thankful as they shook hands and parted company in Nairobi. Jean was already there and the following day they went to shop for a ring. He chose a beautiful sapphire surrounded by two small diamonds which he put on her finger that night after a romantic dinner. They had decided to announce their engagement on Boxing Day, the day after Christmas Day. It was the day her parents had got married and they wanted to have a big party for them. They both felt sad that Lawrence's parents could not be there but they lived in England and it was just too far away.

It seemed the ideal time to talk as they drove from Nairobi to Kampala. The drive was 400 miles over dirt roads and took them through the Kenya Highlands. "I really want to know so much more about your family. Why don't you tell me everything about your life, going back to where you were as a child during the war when we were both children in England?" Jean asked. They talked non-stop all the way from Nairobi to Kampala.

Lawrence was born in Liverpool during the war and lived through the dreadful bombings that rocked their city on a daily basis. His father was a Civil Engineer and was assigned by the Government to build a Gunnery School and runways for aerodromes. He had built a special air raid shelter for the family and they slept in it every night during the bombing which saved his life as an incendiary bomb fell onto his bed one night. His father's job took him all over the country so he made arrangements for the family to move and live near friends in North Wales. His grandmother, mother, and sister were so happy to be out in the beautiful countryside away from the bombing. He and his older sister Winifred were able to run and play outside again. Their mother signed them up for a nearby school, a Convent run by nuns. The rules were very strict and at only 4 years old he had to learn to spell "Mississippi" to be let out of school. He remembered crying over it, but he soon learned it.

Food was very scarce as it was throughout the country, but their father always managed to bring special treats for them when was able to come home. They could pick wild blackberries and their mother would make delicious blackberry pies. At the end of the war they moved back to Upton in Wallasey across the River Mersey from Liverpool. It was very close to the river and he and his friends would stand against the sea wall waiting for a wave to pull them out into the water and then push them back in. He realized afterwards how dangerous that had been and was thankful that his mother never found out.

His brother Jimmy was born at that time, seven years younger than him. They attended good schools but his sister was a brilliant scholar and musician and his reports were mediocre saying satisfactory but could do much better. He managed to pass his final exams and left school at 16. His father arranged for him to apply to the Liverpool Cotton Association for an apprenticeship and he was asked to go before the Board of Directors. He remembered it being one of the scariest things that happened to him in his young life. He stood in front of 16 seated Board members who questioned him for half an hour, he was scared to death.

"Can't imagine you being scared of anything," Jean said. "But then you were still very young."

"Well I've grown up a lot since then and was brave enough to ask you to marry me," he laughed.

"So did you get accepted?"

"Yes I was and for the following two years I learned a lot about cotton." He continued to tell her that he was drafted for military service and had to leave to go to boot camp. At the camp it was referred to as Hades Half Acre by the troops, because it was such extreme training. The cotton company had promised to give him his job back when his two years in the army were completed; however, he had rheumatic fever and after six weeks in hospital was discharged as medically unfit for further military duty and was able to go back to work. He completed his apprenticeship earlier than he had anticipated because of this.

"Looks like we have arrived back in Kampala" he said. "I can't believe we are already here, we have talked nonstop the whole way."

CHAPTER 27

Jean and Lawrence Wedding Day

I t was close to Christmas when they arrived back and Jean's parents had arranged a party for them to celebrate their engagement on Boxing Day. They really liked Lawrence and were looking forward to welcoming him into their family. They had also started to make plans for their wedding, which was going to be in April.

"I think we should have it at the Reception at Lugogo Stadium," Ron said. The Stadium had been opened very recently by President Obote and had some rooms large enough to accommodate the 200 guests they planned to invite.

"Dad, that would be great," Jean said. "It has everything we need."

Wedding plans went underway and she ordered her wedding dress from the same Indian seamstress that her friend had used. It was stunning and she couldn't wait for her wedding day to come. Everything seemed to fall into place and they had even booked their honeymoon at the beach where Lawrence had proposed to her. Lawrence phoned her at the office one morning and she missed the call. As soon as she got back home she called him. Immediately she knew by the tone of his voice that something was really wrong.

"What's happened?" she asked.

"My Dad has passed away," he said.

"Oh I'm so very sorry. Do you need to fly back to England to be with your family, we could delay our wedding."

"Let me think about this and we'll talk this evening," he said. When they met that evening he had decided that they would go ahead with the wedding and they would both fly back to England for their honeymoon to be with his family.

Jean woke up on the day of her wedding with her bridesmaids bringing her breakfast in bed, followed by a flurry of activity. She then showered and they helped her into her wedding dress. After getting her veil into place they put a glass of champagne in her hand, "to calm her nerves," they said. "I can't drink this," she said. "I don't want to wobble down the aisle." They all laughed, but insisted that she should at least have a sip.

Her father came to take her to All Saints Church. This time she was a bride instead of a bridesmaid. Her heart raced as she walked down the aisle towards the man she loved and was going to marry. The Vicar asked them to say their vows and as Lawrence lifted her veil and kissed her the church erupted with clapping and cheering. As they stepped outside they were bombarded with confetti, Jean threw her bouquet to the crowd and they left for their reception. Speeches were made, some serious, but some more colorful by some of the rugby friends. Jean changed into her going away outfit and the newlyweds waited for the Best Man to bring the car round. They were heading to Entebbe where they would spend three nights of their honeymoon at the Lake Victoria Hotel before leaving for England. The car came round the corner, balloons billowing out behind, tin cans rattling along the road, and "Just Married" sprayed over the back window.

It was Lawrence's sports car, an MGB, and his pride and joy. He knew his Best Man had more than enough to drink and he hoped it would arrive in one piece. It was intact to his relief and the proceeded to get into it.

"We can't drive all the way to Entebbe like this," Jean pointed out.

"Why not?" he said. So they drove all the way with cars honking and people leaning out of their car windows congratulating them.

Their three days were blissfully happy as they swam in the lake, enjoyed picnics that the hotel provided for them, and discussed their future together. Lawrence told her that their trip to England was going to cost them a whole year's salary, which meant they would have to both work hard and do some serious saving when they got back.

"It will be worth every penny. I am so looking forward to meeting your family. It has been so hard for them losing your father at this time," Jean said.

CHAPTER 28

They boarded the plane for the long journey. There was just one overnight stop in Malta on the way but the weather was cold, wet, and windy so they couldn't do any sightseeing. It was also cold when they arrived in England, something she soon had to get used to. Despite the weather, a warm welcome awaited them as they arrived at Lawrence's home. His mother was both loving and kind and had redone her bedroom to make it into a honeymoon suite.

"It's not often that a girl gets to spend her honeymoon with her mother-in-law," she said. "We are so pleased to welcome you into our family." Winifred, his sister, took her under her wing too. Jean felt overcome by the generosity of this lovely family who were still struggling with their recent sad loss. Jimmy, Lawrence's younger brother, soon started treating her like a sister and teased her mercilessly. Even the neighbours arrived bringing daffodils. During the next two weeks all Lawrence's Uncles, Aunts, and cousins came to visit. They were all curious to meet his new bride that he had brought all the way from Africa. One of the young cousins said "Why isn't she black? Aren't all people in Africa black?"

Lawrence laughed, "Not all people, but actually her surname was Black before she married me…sorry I have disappointed you," Lawrence smiled at him. They all continued chattering away getting to know each other. She felt so comfortable with all of his relatives, due to the way they made her feel so welcome during their brief stay in England.

CHAPTER 29

Arriving back in Kampala two weeks later Jean was delighted with the house the Company had allocated to them. It was on the same Coffee Estate that Lawrence had lived in as a bachelor and was fully equipped with everything they needed as well as a cook, housekeeper, driver, and gardener all paid for by the Company.

"Hard to believe we have all of this when we actually spent your year's salary on our trip to England and have not a penny in the bank," she said.

"You are so right," Lawrence said. "We now have to get back to work and start saving money."

Jean went back to work with her job at East African Airways and thanks to all the help at home she was able to start entertaining Lawrence's business associates and clients with cocktail and dinner parties. At work one morning she started to suddenly feel sick. Was it the curry they had last night, she wondered as she headed for the bathroom. This happened for the next few mornings and when she told Lawrence he said, "Think you'd better see the doctor."

The doctor confirmed her suspicions. She was about two months pregnant. He offered her anti-nausea pills but she decided not to take them. Hopefully in three months the morning sickness would go away. She was so thankful that she didn't when they discovered months later that these pills could have been Thalidomide, which were causing dreadful deformities in babies. Some babies were being born without some of their limbs because of it. They were both excited about the prospect of becoming parents even though they had hoped it wouldn't be quite so soon.

Lawrence was asked to take over the Company office in Dar es Salaam for a few months. "This will all be great experience for me," he said. "It all adds to my Portfolio for future promotions. You'll have to give up your job here, but possibly you can find another short term one over there." She agreed and hoped they would be able to spend some time at the wonderful beach where Lawrence had proposed to her. She soon managed to find a job with the United States Information Services where they were encouraging Tanganyika to get self-government from the British. Kenya and Uganda were making their transition and when Tanganyika became independent it would make the whole of East Africa an independent country. She had to learn how to write with American spelling instead of British which was quite a challenge, but she enjoyed her job and was kept busy as Lawrence worked long hours in the office.

It was a relief when they were asked to move back to Kampala. She wanted to be near her parents when the baby was born. Jean had planned everything out in advance and told Lawrence that she would put the baby outside in her pram every day under a shady tree just outside their front door for some fresh air.

A beautiful baby girl was born soon after they arrived back, and was delivered by a black nurse at the local Mengo Mission Hospital. This hospital was Uganda's first mission hospital established by Albert Ruskin in 1897. They christened her Julie. As they arrived home from the hospital and walked towards the front door with their precious newborn an enormous snake dropped out of the tree right where the baby's pram would have been.

"Oh no... I won't be putting her out anywhere... she'll be staying close to me. I won't let her out of my sight," Jean said. They were both so thrilled with her and their friends all dropped in to see her each saying, "She looks just like you Jean, or "she looks just like Lawrence." It was a happy time despite some sleepless nights. They had just started to get used to the new baby routine when Lawrence came home with the news that he was being asked to go back to Liverpool. His new position would be Executive Assistant to the Board of Directors to the recently merged company of Ralli Brothers and Coney. "This will be a huge move upwards in my career. I'll be right at the centre of the of the new company as it moves forward." Jean took a deep breath, another move so soon just as they had a new baby.

"When will we be going?" she asked.

"Very soon" he said. "We have to be there in six weeks."

CHAPTER 30

Jean boarded the plane and settled Julie into a carrycot which hung down from the rack above her seat. Lawrence had been delayed at the last minute and so they were travelling on their own. Her brother David would pick them up when they arrived in England. It was a very bumpy trip, but baby Julie slept well as her carrycot rocked back and forth. Lawrence arrived a week later and they left for Liverpool. Jean wanted to live out in the country and after negotiating a loan they bought a small run-down cottage in a small village called Pantymwyn located in North Wales. Lawrence would have to commute an hour each way to the office daily, but they both agreed that this would work well for both of them. They hired a contractor to make improvements to the cottage and settled down to their new life.

It was springtime and beautiful out in the countryside. The newborn lambs were scampering around on the fresh green pastures. The fields were separated by blossoming white Hawthorn bushes and trees blooming with white, pink, and purple flowers. The bluebell woods were Jean's favourites. A carpet of these lovely bluebells stretched out under the trees as far as the eye could see. It seemed as if the whole of nature was lifting up its very soul with joy. Spring turned into summer and Lawrence's mother and sister came to visit them. They were all able to pick blackberries in the fields which his mother made into delicious pies, just like he remembered her doing when he was a little boy. Summer turned to Autumn and the weather turned cooler, and then winter struck. The winds were vicious and then the ice and snow arrived. It was bitterly cold. Their heating in the cottage was minimal. The baby's hot water bottle she had dropped on the floor froze, some flowers froze in the vase, and the sheets froze on the washing line. Trying to manage Julie's diapers and Lawrence's muddy rugby clothes was almost impossible. Lawrence was also having to travel abroad for the company so she was on her own a lot without friends or family. He realized this was not a good situation for her, so they talked and decided to sell the cottage and move nearer to his family. They decided to put it on the market in early spring when it would be looking at its best.

Five months later he came home with some good news. They would not be moving nearer to Liverpool after all but were being sent back to Africa. Jean was so thrilled. "Are we going back to Kampala or Dar es Salaam?" she asked.

"Neither," he said. "We are going to be living in Khartoum in the Sudan."

PART III

Journey into the Desert

CHAPTER 31

The journey was long and the plane seemed to be flying over endless miles of desert. At least, Jean thought, they were traveling together this time. They made a bumpy descent into Khartoum Airport. As soon as they landed the door of the aircraft was opened and the heat poured in along with dust and flies. The heat was suffocating and Jean felt sick. This didn't seem to be the Africa she knew. Large crowds and loud voices speaking in Arabic assailed them as they went through Customs and Immigration, not the friendly faces she was used to, she dearly wished they could be arriving back in Uganda and not here. A driver was sent to pick them up and deliver them to their new home. As they drove up to their house she was pleasantly surprised, perhaps things weren't going to be so bad after all. Two Arab men in traditional long white Galabeyas were waiting at the door for them and ushered them in offering cold orange juice and explaining that they would be their cook and house servants.

"As-salaam-alykum," they both said in Arabic as they grinned from ear to ear, especially when they saw baby Julie. Osman would be their cook and Mohammed was their house servant who appeared to be missing his two front teeth. The house was fully equipped much like their home in Kampala had been. They showed them around and took them out to the garden.

"This is amazing, Lawrence," Jean said. "Can you believe this, we even have a swimming pool." Things were certainly starting to look up. They talked for a long time after dinner assessing their new situation. Lawrence was now Managing Director of the Khartoum Cotton Company which was the second largest exporter of cotton from the Sudan. Cotton represented two thirds of the foreign exchange earnings of the Sudan. This was a big job and he needed Jean to be available to help with entertaining clients from all over the world. "I think we should hire a Nanny and maybe you could get a part time job. We do need to start saving now and this would be a good time to do it." She nodded and agreed, it seemed like a good plan. Once they had settled down and found a Nanny, she would look for a job.

Osman, the cook, produced some excellent meals for them, but Mohammad did not like being told what to do by a woman. He did the laundry and ironed Lawrence's shirts beautifully, but when she saw him fill his mouth with water and blow it through his missing teeth to dampen the shirts she was horrified. He wasn't about to change his method until she got Lawrence to talk to him.

Walking into the kitchen one day with Julie just starting to toddle beside her she spotted an enormous spider right in front of her. She froze and in a panic grabbed Julie and leapt out of the door slamming it behind her. Lawrence arrived home and found her shaking.

"What happened," he said.

"It was a huge spider, the size of my hand in the kitchen," she said.

"You are exaggerating," he said as he opened the kitchen door. The spider had jumped after them and was crushed at the top of the door. They found out later that it was a Camel Spider which capable of giving a very nasty bite.

Jean went to the Souk, the local market with Osman, and found it so interesting to see the different fruits, vegetables, meat, fish, fabric, jewelry, and pottery all for sale. The women wore Toubs, long dresses in different colours, hair covered, and some masking their faces showing only their eyes. Everyone seemed to be shouting at each other as they bartered and argued over sales. Jean had been careful to dress respectfully not showing bare arms or legs which the Muslim faith did not allow. She was beginning to learn so many new things about this country they were now living in. Lawrence hired an Ethiopian Nanny called Elly for them, and Jean managed to find a part time job with the British Council.

One morning she got up early as usual and had breakfast before leaving for work. A strong hot dry wind was blowing and dust was coming in. The sky was darker than normal and she thought it might begin to rain. Suddenly she heard the shouts of the servants,"Haboob coming!" they were yelling. She went into the kitchen and saw Osman running around shutting doors and using sheets to cover the windows.

"What on earth is going on?" she said. He took her arm and pulled her outside.

"Look at the horizon!" he said pointing his finger to where the sky was being obscured by a huge menacing dark red cloud which was moving in their direction. "This is a Haboob, a dust storm which blows in off the desert and can last several hours or even days. We have to cover everything up shut all the doors and windows and stay inside." Lawrence arrived home and they tried to cover everything they could. The sky grew dark as if it were nighttime, but the sky was red and the storm was relentless. The wind sounded like a tornado as it strengthened and they were all enveloped in a cloud of dust. There was nowhere to go to get away from it as the dust swirled around them. They tried to use wet towels to cover themselves, but it still seeped into everything. Several miserable hours passed by as they sheltered in the house. Julie cried herself to sleep eventually and by later that night the storm had passed over them. They showered in the morning and left red muddy sand in the shower. It took several days before they got all the dust out of their hair, ears, and bodies. The house was a disaster and dust was in everything. It took weeks to get it all cleaned up.

"How often do these Haboobs happen?" Jean asked Osman.

"Not too many times." He said but he didn't sound very convincing.

CHAPTER 32

Jean liked the Sudanese people. They seemed to be friendly with no prejudice against Christians living and working in Khartoum; however, she found out through her job that they were at war with the Christians in southern Sudan. The Sudanese Government was a Military dictatorship under General Aboud but was pro-western and welcomed businesses from different countries. They got to know several members of the highly respected Mahdi family through Lawrence's business, and Jean became very friendly with some of their wives. The women had to wear their traditional dress called Toubs outdoors but it was different at home. When Jean visited them they were all in mini-skirts which were all the fashion at the time. She was honoured to be invited to the mourning of one of their fathers who had passed away. She went into a large room in their home where all the women sat in a large circle wailing and ululating, a strange and unusual trilling sound, full of anguish and pain, each time someone new joined the circle. It was a very different tradition and somewhat unnerving but she thought that it was probably so good for them to display such heartfelt emotion. The Muslim faith was very different to Christianity and she wanted to know much more about it. They were so devout and washed their hands and prayed five times a day, where they faced Mecca their spiritual center. Osman and Mohammed allowed Julie to toddle down and be with them when they prayed in the early morning. She mimicked what they were doing and fell on her face as they did jabbering away in her baby talk as they muttered their prayers.

Lawrence decided to buy a motor boat so they could take some trips along the river Nile which ran through the heart of Khartoum. "It will be so relaxing to get away from the office on weekends and we could take some picnics with us," he said. It was a great idea and Jean looked forward to getting away from the stuffy heat of the city. She was pregnant again, and over her early morning sickness. This was going to be such a good change.

This river had so much history attached to it, both in Uganda where she had lived near to the source of the White Nile at Lake Victoria, and now in Khartoum where the Blue River Nile coming from Ethiopia confluenced with the White Nile to make it the longest river in the world. They joined the Sailing Club where they could dock the boat and spent many happy hours on the river. Along the banks they would see Arab traders with their camels and occasionally children at the water's edge collecting water. The Sailing Club was a very old iron gunboat which the famous Gordon of Khartoum had brought up the River in 1884 to rescue a besieged Garrison held by the British. At that time the Sudan was a British Protectorate and the Mahdi, an Arab tribe, were fighting to remove the British from their country. General Gordon was a highly respected British General who had been appointed to take charge of the uprising. He had established a military Garrison in Khartoum after fighting many battles moving troops up the river. When it became apparent that it was necessary to evacuate as many of the women, children, and civilians who were living there, he once again fought his way past the attacks and guns along the riverbanks and rescued 2500 people. The British Government gave him orders not to return again, but knowing his troops and others including missionaries were still under a dire siege, he returned. The Mahdi prevailed and nearly all those living in Khartoum were brutally massacred including General Gordon whose head had been cut off and presented to their leader. This was a radical side to the Muslim faith and Jean realized that it was very different to the Christian belief and the teaching of Jesus which was about love, peace, and forgiveness. She also thought it very ironic that nearly a century later some of her very best friends were the wives of some of the Mahdi family.

CHAPTER 33

A Co-Director of Lawrence's, Mohie-el-Din-el-Bereir, wanted him to see the Suki cotton plantation he owned which was situated three hours away on the banks of the Blue Nile. It was a perfect crop grown in the rich soil of the silt that was washed down every year with the flow of the river. He spent the weekend with him and was given a galabeya to wear on his arrival. He said it was the most comfortable clothing he had ever worn, and they had a very relaxed weekend talking and eating some different Sudanese food. On his return to Khartoum there was a message waiting for him asking him to go to Hong Kong and Japan to meet with some of the Textile Companies and their owners so that they could trade and sell cotton directly to them.

"This will be a great opportunity to meet some of the top businessmen in both countries," he said. "I'll be away for two weeks." Jean realized this was exciting for him, he had always wanted to travel, and what better way to do it than through a business he loved.

"Please be sure to write and let me know what it's like," she said. His first letter arrived after ten days and his description of Hong Kong was so real she almost felt that she was there with him. The view from the Mandarin Hotel where he stayed was over the harbour with ships from all over the world and Chinese Junks weaving in and out between them was fascinating. The sheer number of Chinese living on this small island was overwhelming and when he walked out into the streets it was hard not to bump into people. It was so different to anywhere he had ever been. The efficiency of the way everything seemed to work despite the hustle bustle of the crowds was amazing. He was taken to various restaurants where he learned to eat Chinese food, even Bird's Nest Soup. At a fish restaurant he was made to eat with chopsticks and the business man he was with threatened to feed him if he didn't. He shopped at some of the street markets and bought presents for Jean and Julie in between his meetings. He met with several business owners and managed to create a successful relationship with them. They were pleased with the samples of cotton he had brought with him and made their first orders. He was elated. This had been a very successful trip and they looked forward to doing future business together.

Jean met him at the Airport with one very excited little girl who flung herself at him. It was so good to have him home again, they had missed him so much.

CHAPTER 34

"Guess what? Can you believe it? The Queen is coming to Khartoum on an official visit and we have been invited by the British Embassy to attend an official party for her at Government House," Lawrence said. "She wishes to meet with heads of business companies as well as all Sudanese Government Ministers."

Jean was excited, it was very rare to have an opportunity to meet with the Queen and it would be such a great honour. The visit was going to be in another month though and could well coincide with the birth of their new baby. She would just have to hope for the best and as her due date for delivery came near, and she planned to still go even if she was so heavily pregnant.

The evening arrived and she was already 10 days overdue, but she had made up her mind, this was a once in a lifetime event and she was determined not to miss it.

It was 7 o'clock in the evening and the gardens of the Embassy were bright with lights everywhere as well as focused on a curved staircase coming down from the balcony on the second floor of the building. Guests were assigned to different areas. Lawrence to the business side and Jean had been given a chair at the end next to some very elderly Veterans of World War 1 who were wearing all their medals. It was a fairytale scene Jean thought as she waited to be introduced to Her Royal Highness. There was a sudden hush as guests were asked to be quiet and as Queen Elizabeth stepped out onto the balcony wearing a beautiful gown and her tiara as the band started to play 'God Save the Queen'.

She slowly descended down the staircase with the Governor at her side and was directed to the line of old soldiers. Jean started to panic, she was first in line and as she heaved herself off the chair to stand up. She knew that she was supposed to curtsy as that was the proper protocol, but she thought she might fall over if she did. The Queen of course was very gracious and motioned for her to sit down and after being introduced to her moved on along the lines of people waiting for their introduction. Jean noticed she spent longer with Lawrence than with most people there and afterwards he told her that the Queen was really interested in cotton and asked him a lot of questions about the industry. He was surprised that she was so well versed and had obviously been briefed in detail.

CHAPTER 35

After all the excitement died down Jean waited expectantly for her baby to arrive, but nothing seemed to be happening. "I have the solution," Lawrence said. "I'm going to take you out into the desert over some bumpy roads and shake you up a bit, that just might do the trick." They went out in the early evening to avoid the heat but Jean felt so hot and uncomfortable they didn't go very far before she asked to go home. That night she tossed and turned in her sleep having nightmares, but in the early hours of the morning her waters broke and she knew that the baby was finally on the way. Lawrence took her along with Julie to the Catholic Mission Hospital which was run by Catholic nuns. It had such a good reputation for taking care of patients and was much safer than using the local hospital which was far from ideal. The nuns rushed her immediately into the delivery room after they examined her. "This baby is about to be born quickly!" said the nun. This was a huge relief to Jean as the nuns did not believe in giving any form of pain killer. Forty-five minutes later her baby arrived, another beautiful little girl who they named Sally Anne Katrina. The name Katrina was the name of the baby that Jean had wanted to adopt when she was Nursing at the hospital in England.

They were all thrilled to have a new addition to their family. "It worked," Lawrence said. "We know what to do if we have any more overdue babies, just head for the desert!" Jean stayed in the hospital for a few days but was very disturbed by the screams of women having their babies and the Mullah in the Mosque close by who was loudly calling out prayers several times a day to the people. The screams of the women were unnerving so Jean asked one of the nuns why they made such a terrible sound.

"You have no idea what these women have been through," she said. "In their tradition they believe that girls have to be circumcised usually soon after birth and before they are five years old. This is to make them acceptable for them to get a husband. In the villages they are held down by a family member as an old woman who has used this practice for years cuts much of the outside and inside of the vagina away usually with a dirty razor blade. They are then stitched together with thorns leaving just a small hole for them to be able to empty their bladder and allow their menstrual flow when they get older. They have no numbing or anesthesia while this is being done to them, and it has to be agonizing. Their legs are then tied together for several days to stop the bleeding. It is the most barbaric and dreadful tradition that has gone on for many years, not only in the Middle East, but also in parts of Africa and other countries around the world. Now that people have come to know about it there are many groups involved in trying to put an end to it. You can't imagine what terrible pain they are going through when they are having babies and we do everything we can to help them." Jean was horrified and speechless, the cruelty was beyond comprehension. She found herself saying a prayer for these poor women whenever she heard the screams and held her own baby close in thankfulness that she was able to have a normal birth.

CHAPTER 36

Arriving back home she found a whirlwind of activity going on in the house. The President of the Liverpool head office was arriving in a few days and bringing several very important clients with him. Lawrence had to arrange meetings with several companies, take them on a tour of the cotton growing areas, and entertain a lot of them at home. Cocktail and dinner parties had to be arranged and Jean had to start organizing it all very quickly. She knew how important this was for Lawrence and the company, but she had to juggle all of this along with her new baby and her job. She was very thankful for her Nanny, Elly, who was proving to be so valuable. She was so good with the children and managed to settle Julie down when her baby sister seemed to be getting all the attention.

Everything started to fall into place and they met their six guests off the plane and took them to the hotel where they would be staying during their visit. Lawrence had arranged a trip for them the following morning. He thought it would be a good idea to take them out along the river on the boat. It would be relaxing for them and they would have a chance to get over their jet lag before starting on all the business. They left early in the morning before the heat of the day and his President and clients were really enjoying this lovely trip down the river Nile. They were amazed at all the different sights and sounds which were so new to them. They chugged along slowly to get the best views and Lawrence turned the boat around to make their way back.

"I'll put my foot down going back," he said. "We'll have a nice breeze to keep us cool." Everyone was chatting happily when suddenly the boat came to an abrupt and violent stop. They were all shaken and nearly fell overboard, one client losing his glasses. "Can you believe it?" Lawrence said, "We've hit a sand bank." These sandbanks come up in different places occasionally and are underwater so you can't see them. "I am so sorry," he felt mortified. This was terrible and no way to make an impression on these very important people. Even worse he now had to ask them to get out of the boat so they could push it off the sand bank. They took off their shoes and all heaved and pushed until the boat was released and they were able to make their way slowly back up the river. Fortunately they all got out laughing and saying that this was one trip that they would remember. The rest of the visit went really well and some good business was done. All the parties were a success and Lawrence's boss congratulated him on the outcome of this visit.

CHAPTER 37

"I'm going to ask my Mum if she would like to fly over to see us," Lawrence said. "She could come here and then go on to Uganda and see your parents."

"I think that would be great." Jean said. "She'll really enjoy being able to see her grandchildren." He booked her flights and gave her some instructions as this was going to be her very first trip abroad, as well as her first flight ever. They were all so excited to see her when she got off the plane and she said how wonderful her flight had been. Soaring up above the earth and flying through clouds had been an extraordinary experience for her. She wrapped her arms around them all, giving Julie the biggest hug and holding baby Sally for the first time. They tried not to make too many plans, but friends kept coming in to welcome her and of course they took her out on the river.

The Mahdi family invited them to a special dinner at their mud Palace in Omdurman, the historical center of the Mahdi a century earlier. They had so much respect for their elders and it was a great honour for her to be invited to their Palace. Both her and Jean dressed carefully in caftans with long sleeves for the night of the dinner. They did not want to be disrespectful in any way. They drove to Omdurman and were greeted at the door of the Palace and led into a large room full of men dressed in galabiuyas. There was a lattice style wall on one side of the room and all of the women were behind it. Lawrence's Mum and Jean were the only women in the room. The table was set with gold plates all carefully arranged and they were asked to sit down. Orange juice and water were served, no wine or alcohol which was against their religion. The men spoke both in Arabic and English and welcomed them warmly. Lawrence's Mum felt that she had been set down in a scene from Arabian nights; she was speechless, it was so unreal. The dinner was food that she had never had before but she tried everything and enjoyed most of it. They toasted her both in Arabic and English and she thanked them graciously. It was a night to remember, and it was one of the highlights of her visit.

CHAPTER 38

It had been a very busy few weeks and when things quietened down Jean felt tired and listless. It was hard to go to work every day and leave the children even in the very capable hands of Elly. She had recently found an English boyfriend and wanted to take more time off. She asked Jean if she could bring him over for a meeting with Lawrence, so Jean organized dinner for the four of them. After dinner he asked Lawrence if he could speak to him privately so the two of them went outside. "I am being sent back to England very soon and I want to take Elly with me. Can I have your permission to ask her to marry me?" he said. Lawrence was taken back, this wasn't an easy question and not one that a 28 year old would normally be asked. It would also mean taking Elly to a new country where she might find herself among strangers in a totally different culture. He was also not convinced that this man would follow through on his promises to Elly once he got back to England; however, he knew it really wasn't up to him.

"Please think this through very carefully," he said. "And don't raise her hopes and let her down." Elly was so happy and excited at the thought of going to England to join him and get married. It would be a huge step forward for a young Ethiopian woman who had grown up in a small village in relative poverty. She agreed to marry him and he said he would send for her as soon as he had settled down back in England.

CHAPTER 39

Lawrence scheduled a visit to some of the East European Communist countries to sell cotton to the Trading Companies in Poland, Bulgaria, Czechoslovakia, Hungary, and Romania. He was going to be away for two weeks. "Why don't you go and visit your parents in Uganda while I'm gone," he said. "You haven't been feeling too good lately and a change would do you good, plus your parents would love to see their grandchildren." Jean jumped at the idea, she had been tired and a bit depressed and the doctor had told her that she was suffering from postpartum depression which can sometimes happen after the birth of a baby.

Once more Jean boarded a plane, this time with two children, for a flight to Entebbe. As they descended to the airport Jean saw the familiar sights of Lake Victoria, the red earth, and the brilliant green vegetation with banana and papaya trees. Her heavy heart started to lift, she was coming home to the country she loved so much. Her parents were there to meet them and they were all swept up in hugs and kisses. The children settled down very quickly and enjoyed the spoiling that only grandparents can give. Her Mum, Florence, arranged a lovely curry party and invited a lot of their old friends who still lived there. Jean's spirit soared once again and she felt so much better. The time seemed to pass by far too quickly, but she was also missing Lawrence. She knew that those countries he was in were very Communist and also very poor. There was no way of communicating with each other, so she just had to pray that he would stay safe.

She arrived back in Khartoum a few days before he returned so she was able to meet him at the airport when he arrived back.

"You look so tired. Was it a tough trip?" Jean asked.

"It has been a very tough trip. It was one of the worst places I have ever been to." Lawrence responded. "When I arrived in each country everything seemed drab and grey. Even the people were very poorly dressed and seemed to be struggling and the few cars on the road were very old. Of course going there in November didn't help as there were no leaves on the trees and the wind and icy rain made it worse. Food was available, but shortages often happened and it was very expensive. The Managers tried to do their best but the companies were all State-owned so they had limited powers to be able to trade. The last country I visited was in Poland and the Managing Director was a women which was very unusual. She told me that women had taken over many of the jobs that had always been for men as six million men had died in the war. It was very sad to see what had happened in all these countries and what difficult lives they were leading." He was so glad to be home again with the family and although the weekdays at the office were long they were able to enjoy their weekends on the river.

CHAPTER 40

S everal months passed by and they were feeling happy and settled in Khartoum. They knew that they wouldn't be staying there forever and often friends that they had made were moved elsewhere by their companies. It was always hard to see them go as they felt more like family than friends when they were all living in a foreign country without family. Phone calls did not work very well so most people communicated with their families by letter. The phone rang and Jean was surprised when she heard her Father's voice on the other end of the line. "I have some really bad news to tell you," he said. "There has been a military coup in Uganda and Idi Amin has ousted President Obote while he was at a Commonwealth Prime Ministers Conference in Singapore. President Obote has gone into exile in Tanzania. Some of his soldiers were still trying to put up a fight in different parts of the country. A group of drunk soldiers drove into Spadge and Beetle's camp one night dragged Beetle out and beat him to death. Spadge was raped mercilessly and then murdered too. One of the Catholic Missionary Fathers who was a friend of theirs had gone there the next day and found the horrific scene. Their servants had all fled and the dogs had been shot."

"Unbelievable," Jean said, tears in her eyes. "I can't believe they did this to them… it's barbaric."

"It is. Your mother and I are concerned about what is going to happen next. Hundreds of people have been rounded up, tortured, and killed. Dead bodies have been found floating in Lake Victoria and

President Idi Amin is now threatening to nationalize companies and throw all the Indian families out of the country. They originally came to Uganda many years ago from India to build the railways and had stayed on afterwards and developing businesses. They now owned many of the large sugar plantations.

"Surely they can't do that. They are such huge contributors to the finances of the country... it would be a disaster."

"I know. The place will be in an enormous uproar and I think that we should move back to England. It will be sad to leave, but we have had many happy years here and it is time to move on."

Jean told Lawrence the sad news that evening and they both reminisced about the happier times they had spent with her family in Uganda. He was shocked at the news about Beetle and Spadge. He had met them several times and Beetle had celebrated with him and Jean's Mum and Dad on the night of Julie's birth. They had celebrated a bit too well and turned up to visit Jean in the hospital the next day with terrible hangovers. She had no sympathy. "You should try having a baby," she said, "hangovers don't compare."

"I have a feeling we might not be staying here much longer either," Lawrence said. "Our Liverpool Office is wanting someone to take over the business in the Far East as well as some European business, and I may get asked to do it. It would mean moving back to England. How would you feel about it?"

Jean laughed, " I remember when we first met and you told me how ambitious you were, and you also told me that we would probably have to move a lot so I knew what I was letting myself in for. Of course I'd be happy to move back. We would be near the grandparents and the girls and I would all love it."

He turned out to be right. Two months later he was asked to go back again to take up a new position as Sales Manager of the Far East and Turkey. This would be a major job and would involve a lot of travel to visit companies and clients in all these countries.

They prepared for their departure and were invited to lots of farewell parties. Jean's Mahdi girlfriends went to great lengths to hire a Paddle Steamer to take her out on the river to say goodbye. She was overcome and tearful at the thought of leaving these dear friends they had become a very special part of her life. She had learned a lot about their faith and despite their differences they had a lot in common and they never tried to convert her to their way of believing. Jean's Christian faith was still on shaky ground and, even though she prayed she still had many unanswered questions about her own belief.

A letter addressed to Lawrence arrived from Elly's English fiancé. It was as they had feared. He wanted to tell her that he no longer wanted her to come to be with him. She was heartbroken, it was such a letdown especially as the family were all going back there. She pleaded with them to take her with them, but they knew that it wouldn't work. They felt a lot of responsibility for her and managed to find her another job. It was a difficult decision, but they knew that they had done the right thing.

CHAPTER 41

A few days of rain cooled down the intense heat and made them all feel better. "Why don't we ride out into the desert one last time?" Lawrence said. "It's unlikely that we will be coming back here and they do say that the desert blooms when it rains." They packed up the car with plenty of drinks and snacks for the children and took off for the day. As they drove out of the town and towards the desert they couldn't believe their eyes. This was amazing, a transformation had taken place and beautiful wild flowers had sprung up everywhere. It was ablaze with color. Even the children who disliked being cooped up in a car were excited. "Can we get out and pick some?" they asked.

"Yes," Jean said, "why don't you pick some and take them back for Elly as she is feeling sad right now." They jumped out of the car.

"Hold on a minute, we need to be very careful, because we know that there are rattlesnakes and spiders out there. So I will go ahead of you and we won't go far from the car," Lawrence warned them. Jean watched them as they trod carefully in their father's footsteps. Her thoughts drifted. How could it be that these tiny seeds had lain dormant for so long and then could burst through the dry and arid desert to produce such a display of incredible beauty. What power lay behind this, was it the power of God which gave life to everything even the tiniest seed to blossom when the time was right? They all came back interrupting her thoughts with excited chatter and showing her all the flowers they had managed to pick.

"I just have one more trip I must do before we leave," Lawrence said. "I want to check out the Abyan Cotton Scheme in Aden, they grow some very good cotton and I may be able to buy some from them. It's situated on the Gulf of Aden in south Yemen on the Red Sea. It's not a particularly safe place to visit, but I should be well protected by the owners of the Scheme who are very keen to do business. Aden had been a British Protectorate since 1837 and was an important trading hub and coaling station after the Suez Canal had opened. It was now going through political upheaval and Communists were trying to take it over. "It makes sense to go now as it's a relatively short distance from Khartoum and would only take a few days." Jean agreed that it would be better than going there soon after they arrived back in England.

"Stay safe, and come home in one piece," Jean said.

Arriving back ten days later he had successfully achieved what he had gone for, but not without being in a very dangerous situation. Arriving in Aden he had to travel by taxi 39 miles to the Abyan Cotton Scheme along a beach as there were no roads. As they drove along an armed soldier suddenly jumped out in front of them with his gun raised and pointing it directly at them. The taxi driver screeched to a halt and told Lawrence to duck. They were both terrified, because this was a lawless country and they didn't know if they were about to be shot. He walked over to them demanding that they got out of the car. Speaking in Arabic to the driver he asked where they were planning to go and what they were doing there. The driver eventually turned to Lawrence and said, "He was actually trying to save us as the beach has been mined and we would have been blown up if he hadn't stopped us." The soldier then directed them on a path around the minefield and they were able to continue their journey safely.

They left for England soon after he arrived back and as they parted company with all their friends and associates, they felt sad. It had been an extraordinary few years in this country. They had learned so much about the warmth of the Sudanese people and would cherish the memories they would take away with them.

PART IV

Travels Around the World

CHAPTER 42

Borderhouse

The wind howled and the rain pounded down on the rooftop waking her from a dreamless sleep. For a few moments she tried to figure out where she was until the realization came to her. It was their first night in the new home they had bought in England two months after they had arrived back from Khartoum. She pulled up the covers and snuggled closer to Lawrence who put his arm around her. "Storm wake you up?" he said. "I expect we'll have to get used to this English weather again." It had been a hectic two months house hunting and finding their way around the village they decided to live in. It was an ideal place to live… good schools, medical centers, shops, and Liverpool was a short commute for Lawrence. He would have to take the Ferry over the River Mersey or drive through an underground tunnel each day to get to work, but home would be more out in the country and away from the city. They had found a big old house built in 1890 made of sandstone which they immediately fell in love with. It was run down and needed a lot of love and care but it would be a perfect place for their family.

Lawrence soon found out that he would be travelling extensively. They wanted him to go to many different countries to both buy and sell cotton, and they would expect him to entertain lots of business visitors from all over the world.

"Do you think you can handle this?" he said. "You'll have to get the house in shape, get the girls into schools pretty much on your own. I could be turning up in the evening with all sorts of people so we have to find a good babysitter. We no longer have servants so it will all be on you."

"Remember you told me early on that our life would be different and full of change and excitement. I chose to marry you so I can manage this," Jean replied.

The days were filled with frantic activity as the general contractor worked on the inside of the house. They were careful to keep its character and found all sorts of hidden treasures as the work progressed. Julie and Sally were 8 and 5 and pleaded for a puppy, so they bought a gorgeous golden Labrador and named her Susie. She quickly added to the chaos of all the work being done on the house. They found a gardener who was able to make them a fishpond in the garden and they had carefully picked out the fish and plants they liked. The pond looked beautiful and they felt very proud of it, but Susie decided to pull out all the fish and plants and swim in it. It was a muddy mess and Jean had a hard time trying to console two very tearful little girls. Susie also nearly burnt the house down after Jean had left a pot of chicken stock on the back burner of the cooker. The knobs were on the front and she jumped up and managed to turn on the one underneath the pan while they were all out. Fortunately the Contractor came by and found the kitchen full of smoke and the recently redecorated kitchen on fire. He rescued the dog and put out the fire, but the kitchen had to be done all over again, just as they thought they had finished with the months of remodeling. Perhaps a dog had not been such a great idea, but they loved her anyway.

"You must have run out of the door and left it on by mistake," Lawrence said. "The dog couldn't have done that." Three weeks later the same scenario happened with some friends and he finally believed her.

Lawrence was traveling frequently to Hong Kong, Australia, China and the Far East and was usually away for two and sometimes three weeks at a time. Jean found it harder than she thought and missed him a lot. He told her about all the places and people that he had met and the excitement of opening up the market in Communist China at the time of the Cultural Revolution in 1970. The only progress that had been made from the Communist takeover in 1949 was an increase in the cloth ration from 1 yard per person annually to 2 yards and they had a cotton crop failure on their hands. Chairman Mao Tse Tung made the decision that they could not afford to reduce the cloth ration and they would have to trade with the enemy, the United States of America. As this could not be done directly, the Chinese asked Lawrence if their Company could arrange for this to be done. Subsequently he was able to purchase from the American Cotton Cooperatives. Two hundred and fifty thousand tons of cotton which were shipped on twenty three charter ships to various ports in China. This was the largest transaction ever done which resulted in Lawrence's Company, Ralli Bros and Coney, becoming one of the three top cotton merchants in the world.

When he arrived in Peking there was only one hotel and it was clear to him that everyone was spying on him as well as each other. No one would look him in the eye or conduct a conversation. There were no private cars on the road and ten million people on bicycles. As he walked back from the office one day he found himself in the middle of a huge marching crowd. He was handed a little red book acclaiming Mao Tse Tung which had all his disciplinary rules in it. He had it translated and Jean and was horrified. The people were under a strict regime and had no freedom whatsoever. Mao Tse Tung had originally based his ideology on Russian Communism and the Maoist regime came about with the Cultural Revolution which would rid China of the old ways of behaviour, their customs, habits, thoughts, and ideas. The people would all have to be retrained to only think and say what the Party taught and the Red Guard were formed to enforce this. Educated people such as professors, teachers, doctors, artists, and many others were sent for retraining and made to do menial work in the country. He was a cruel and Authoritarian leader who required the population to worship him. It made Jean think of Adolf Hitler and the Nazi's horrific rule during World War 2.

"Did you feel safe there?" she asked.

"Yes," he said. "They badly needed the cotton to clothe the people and wanted this deal to go through, but I felt very relieved when I was able to leave."

CHAPTER 43

Jean and Lawrence with the Girls

"I have to go to Hong Kong again soon, but I would like you to come with me," Lawrence told Jean one morning as he was getting ready for work. Jean was taken back, because she wasn't expecting this.

"How can I? What about the girls and you know that I am three months pregnant."

"Well you are over your morning sickness and feeling good. As for the girls you have two choices…you can either leave them with the babysitter or you can bring them with you." She didn't hesitate. This would be a wonderful trip for all of them and she would get to meet some of the business associates he had so often told her about. He found a local Chinese restaurant and took them there for dinner for a whole week teaching them all how to master chopsticks. Julie and Sally were both very excited about going on a trip with their Daddy and took it all very seriously. Lawrence said that he would be leaving ahead of them, but he knew Jean was capable of coping with the long flight.

They would be making three stops en route on this 24 hour journey including Tehran. The flight to Teheran was uneventful and the girls behaved very well and had games and books to keep them occupied on the way. They started their descent into the airport and as the plane touched down there was a tremendous thump and screeching as the plane bumped and skidded from side to side for a long time before coming to a stop. Something was very wrong this was not a normal landing. Somebody screamed and Jean grabbed the girls hands and held them very tight. The plane finally came to a halt leaning to one side and the Captain's voice came over the loudspeaker, "Sorry about that folks….that was a very rough landing, I think we have burst some tires and we will all have to stay on the plane until the authorities here tell us what to do."

Two hours later they were allowed to go to a waiting bus which took them to an isolated building with one toilet and no other facilities. It was evening and getting cooler, but the heat was stifling in the crowded building. Soldiers with guns were posted outside and no one was allowed out. Sweet sticky orange juice was handed to them, but there was no water available. They felt like prisoners. They all had their passports inspected and were questioned by some men in plain clothes. They were finally told that the plane had burst several tires and they would have to wait for replacements to be flown out. Both girls started to throw up after drinking the juice and Jean went to the door and asked if she could go outside with the children. "No," said the guard and shut the door firmly in her face.

One of Lawrence's co-workers happened to be on the plane and saw her dilemma and went to the door. He talked to the soldier and offered him some money and came back to Jean. "He will let you go out with the children, but you'll have to sit on the curb there is nothing out there." Jean was so grateful to breathe in the fresh air after the stifling heat inside, but as they sat there she felt the whole thing was very surreal and threatening. Eight hours later they were all herded back onto the bus and boarded the plane. It was a huge relief and she found out later that there had been unrest in Teheran and they had been checking and imprisoning some foreigners who they thought were spies. The Captain, once again, asked them to fasten their seat belts as they made their approach into Hong Kong Airport. As the plane descended it was another tense moment as the plane seemed to fly through a narrow space with apartment buildings on either side, so close that they could see the people inside and washing hanging out on some of the buildings. Finally they landed in Hong Kong Airport and she breathed a sigh of relief as they went through Customs and Immigration and met Lawrence on the other side. In his usual humorous way he said, "Where have you been... you've been keeping me waiting?" Jean glared at him but in seconds they all threw their arms round each other. She was so thankful to finally have arrived safely.

They stayed with friends in their large apartment who were part of the Company. They had known Pat and Paul before they had been sent to Hong Kong, so it was great to catch up with them. "There is so much to see here," Pat said. "I'll take you on a tour round and then let you loose to go and explore." They were amazed at the huge number of Chinese people on the streets busily running around, it felt quite overwhelming after living in a small village in England. Shopkeepers came out of the many shops and tried to persuade them to come in and buy. Street vendors were cooking on small carts and pushed food in front of their faces trying to make a sale and cars and rickshaws filled the roads. It looked chaotic but everyone seemed to know where they were going. Pat took them down into the street markets which were vibrant with colour and had everything imaginable for sale. Designer watches, clothes, shoes, and handbags which were cheap and almost exactly like the real thing. The girls wanted jeans and went behind a curtain to try them on. Determined to get them as tight as possible they both laid on the floor to try and wriggle into them. They tried some different Chinese foods but didn't like it. It wasn't anything like the food they had at the English Chinese restaurants.

Lawrence wanted Jean to meet some of the Textile owners that he was dealing with, so he organized some dinner parties and the owner of the biggest Textile Company invited them and the children for dinner at his home. They drove up to his beautiful home on the Peak, the highest point in Hong Kong where the views were spectacular. It was a Chinese designed home with a stunning interior and exquisite furnishings. After welcoming them in and introducing them to his extended family, he took them on a tour showing them all the many different rooms including two large dining rooms.

"This is where the children will eat. I want them to dine with my grandchildren," he informed them. After drinks in the sitting room Julie and Sally were led away to meet the grandchildren as the adults moved into the main dining room. Sally looked pleadingly at Jean, clung tightly to her hand and wanted to stay with her.

"C'mon Sal," Julie said. "We have to go… I'll take you." The main dining room had a huge round table and as they were seated wine was poured and a toast was made to them. The food started to arrive and a small amount was served on gold plates, each one a work of art. They described what they were and some were delicious, but Jean had a hard time with some. Birds Nest soup which apparently was a Chinese delicacy made from the spittle of tiny Swiftlet birds and cooked to make soup was not easy to eat. The broiled snake was another, but she didn't want to offend these important hosts so she did her best. She had mastered the art of eating with chopsticks but these were gold tipped and much more slippery than the plastic ones she had practiced with. She was relieved when the final dish was brought in, it was a whole small roasted pig with perfectly done crackling. It was put in the centre of the table with its snout pointed towards Lawrence who was the honoured guest.

Afterwards desserts were served and then they all retired back to the main room. The children were brought in and it was obvious that Sally had been crying. Julie whispered in Jean's ear, "We didn't like the food and the grandchildren weren't very friendly and spoke to each other in Chinese." Sally perked up as they got into the Chauffer driven car which was waiting outside to take them back.

"This is a nice taxi, Daddy." she said.

"It is," Lawrence said. "This happens to be a Rolls Royce."

A few days later they all flew back to England together and were expecting to be picked up at Heathrow airport by the Company plane. They had realized as they flew into London that the weather was bad as they had to stay buckled up for the last part of the journey. "Weather not too good," the Company pilot said to them, "but hopefully we should fly out of it quite quickly." They scrambled aboard the plane, a twin engined Cessna, as a bolt of lightning followed by a crack of thunder made them feel very nervous. "No worries I've flown through worst storms than this...just sit back and relax," he said. They took off as torrential rain started to pummel the plane and heavy winds seemed to lift them violently up and down. The pilot swore a few times, "Didn't expect these cross winds....just hope we get through them before we go in to land in Liverpool." The weather started to improve and they finally landed safely after a really frightening flight and were so relieved to finally be back home.

CHAPTER 44

Six months later Jean went into the local hospital on her due date, this baby wasn't going to keep her waiting like Sally had and another beautiful baby came into the world. A little boy this time which pleased Lawrence as he felt he was beginning to be outnumbered by girls and wanted a boy who would watch football matches with him, especially Liverpool FC, and in time they could play golf together. They named him James after Lawrence's father and when he took the girls to the hospital to see him they were absolutely thrilled to have a new baby brother.

"Can we take him home with us?" they asked.

"Yes, of course we can and you'll be able to help me look after him," Jean said. They couldn't wait to get back to school the next day to tell their teachers and friends about the addition to their family.

Lawrence decided to buy them a holiday home on the Isle of Anglesey in North Wales. "It will be a great get away for us all. With our busy lives having so many business clients and organizing conferences, not to mention all my travelling, it will be great to be able to take time off and head for a beach," he said. "Beside the fact that when I am away you can take the children and the dog there at weekends.

It would be the ideal place for them to have as their family grew. They found a charming little cottage in Rhosneigr in North Wales overlooking the sea and close to the beach. It was only a three hour drive away and Lawrence would be able to fly down on their aircraft to spend weekends with them. They soon made friends with some of the other families who lived nearby and spent many happy hours together during the summer months. It helped too with some of the loneliness that Jean felt when Lawrence was away on long business trips. As they sat on the beach one lovely warm summers day she watched Julie and Sally run up and down the beach collecting shells and other treasures which they shared and traded with their friends. Baby Jamie, as the girls had decided to call him, was trying to crawl and finding it frustrating in the soft sand. He also kept trying to eat it so had to be watched very carefully. He had no problem with destroying the girls sandcastles so they gave up trying to play with him and went to swim instead. Susie the Lab had her own friends and would run in and out of the water with them, always coming back to thoroughly shake herself and demanding to be towel dried. They had brought a picnic with them and as Jean started to get their sandwiches out Sally said she wanted to go to the bathroom. She gave her the key to the cottage and let her go on her own for the first time. It was so close by and she felt safe to let her go. She soon came back and they all settled in for their picnic.

Later that afternoon the wind started to come up and they packed up to go home. Susie had disappeared and didn't come back to any of their shouts. "She'll come when she's ready. She knows her way back so we don't need to worry, where is the key?" Jean said. They looked at Sally who said she had put it on the towel. The towels had already been picked up and shaken to get the sand out. They all dug around in the sand but it was like looking for a needle in a haystack. How on earth could they get back into the cottage everything had been locked up and there was no one to ask for help? They walked past some of the neighbours' houses but most of them were out. Dusk was falling fast and she spotted a light in one of the windows and went and knocked on the door. A man came out and as she started to explained their predicament Susie suddenly broke through the gathering darkness and ran up to them barking fiercely at the man who shrank back through the door. Jamie started to cry and Julie said, "Yuck Mum, Susie really stinks!" Jean knocked on the door again and shouted, "Please help us we are locked out of our house, we will control the dog." He opened the door again and walked over to their house with them where he spotted a window open slightly at the top. Using his penknife and some string he was able to reach through the gap and raise the latch on the window and got Julie to climb in and open the front door.

"By the way…your dog smells horrible. We sometimes have dead sheep on the beach and dogs love to roll in anything like that," he said to them casually as he left.

CHAPTER 45

Lawrence was still away when they returned home from the beach. He had gone to Afghanistan with a colleague to track down a cotton crop and was unable to contact her. She knew they would be traveling through the Hindu Kush mountain area where communication by phone would be almost impossible. The country was under the control of the Afghan King,d but still she was very unsettled by the lawlessness of the different tribes who wanted to depose him. Poppies were their primary crop which created huge financial wealth for the country as it fed into the drug trade. They also had some very good small cotton crops which they needed to sell, but it would be very difficult for them to find out exactly where this cotton could be located.

Jean felt concerned, but she knew Lawrence loved the adventure of going to new countries and she had to wait until he came home to hear all about it. Three weeks later she had a call from him. "Can you come and pick me up from Manchester Airport. I can't wait to get home," Lawrence said. He was exhausted. It had been a long and tiring journey as they had travelled for eighteen days from Kabul to Mazari Sharif and on to Kunduz through the Salang Pass which at 12,723 feet was the highest mountain pass in the world. Their only means of travel was in a very old taxi which struggled up the rocky mountainside. Finally reaching Kunduz, they met with the four owners of the largest cotton farms and started on some very tough negotiations to purchase their crops. Ten days later they came to an agreement, but this then also had to be settled with the Minister of Agriculture in Kabul. Finally the deal

JEAN PRESTON

was agreed and the Minister invited them to go to a Buzkashi game that was being held in honour of the King's Birthday. The Buzkashi games originally came to Afghanistan from China and Mongolia during the 10th Century and were played by rival villages across the steppes of the Hindu Kush. Teams of ten horses galloped in fierce competition to pick up the carcus of a dismembered goat or small calf to drop it in the circle of the opposing team. The players carried whips in their teeth which they could transfer to their hand to fend off other horses but were not allowed to whip other riders. They were strong and agile men who could lean over to capture the carcus while riding at breakneck speed and turning their horses instantly. It was a magnificent display of horsemanship and riders and he had felt very honoured to have been invited to such an important event.

After his return, they all sat round the dinner table and talked the children. They told him their stories about their friends, school, and sports that they were now involved in. It was so good to be a family together again. "I have brought presents....so we'll open them once you've helped your mother to help with the washing up," he said. With unusual enthusiasm they couldn't wash the dishes fast enough. He had always managed to find traditional dolls for the girls from each country he visited. They were thrilled with each addition to their collection and proudly showed them off to their friends. Jamie had an Afghan drum to add to his collection of African drums. He also had an Australian Didgeridoo brought back from a business trip that both parents had gone on. He had brought Jean a beautiful silver Afghan necklace inlaid with Lapis Lazuli, emerald, and alexandrite stones. She was thrilled and he told her that he had bought it from one of the wives of the men he had met in Kabul. She owned a small jewelry business and wanted to sell her jewelry overseas. She asked him if his wife would be interested in trying to do this for her and gave him her business card to pass on to Jean. She took the card as he fastened the necklace round her neck. It really was a very different and lovely hand maid piece of jewelry.

A few days later she picked up the card again and thought about the possibility of working with this woman to help her sell her jewelry. Lawrence said he would be willing to purchase the jewelry as well as

116

some hand embroidered sheepskin waistcoats if she wanted to start a business. She felt this would be a very exciting new venture for her, so she phoned her friend Daphne who owned a clothing shop. Over a long lunch they discussed this and Jean asked her if she would be her partner in a new business. She agreed and they started to plan how they would market these Afghan products and decided to call their new company Oriental Fashions. All the paperwork was put in place and they sent their orders to Afghanistan. As soon as the jewelry and waistcoats arrived they set out to contact stores and make some sales. It was hard work getting the business off the ground, but they enjoyed the challenge. They soon began to sell to clients and shops. They both had young families and so took turns to drive them to school and pick them up. Just as they began to feel confident about ongoing sales they had a phone call from one of the shops telling them that the two Afghan waistcoats they had purchased were starting to smell. Highly embarrassed they immediately went to pick them up. What could have gone wrong? This hadn't happened before? Taking them home they put them in the garage where they had several waistcoats hanging on a rail. None of them seemed to smell, but the ones they had brought home certainly did.

"Maybe we should treat the inside part of the sheepskin using talcum powder," Jean said. It seemed like a silly idea but worth a try. They used the powder on all the waistcoats and after a few days all of them, even the ones that had been returned, smelt really good. After brushing them down really well they hung them out in the fresh air and wondered if they dared try to sell them to any more shops. After all only two of their previous sales had come back. Other than the two that were returned, they decided to risk selling the rest of their inventory. They managed to sell them all. There were further orders, but they decided it was safer to just continue with the jewelry which was proving to be quite successful.

At the very least it was helping an Afghan woman to promote her business. Most women there were under strict control of their husbands or fathers and were not allowed to do anything outside of the home. This was a centuries old Muslim teaching which was deeply embedded in their faith where women had no rights whatsoever. Their husbands, who were usually much older men, were chosen for them by their fathers. They often had several wives and were able to divorce them by simply saying "I divorce thee" three times. They were then thrown out and mostly not accepted back into their own families. Jean felt so sorry for them and was really thankful she had been born into a western Christian civilization.

It did make her think though about her own beliefs as a Christian. She remembered the time when she was a child at school and the American missionary who had terrified her, and Molly when he put his hands on their heads and asked if they believed in Jesus and wanted to be saved. They both said yes very quickly because he said they would go to hell if they didn't. Neither of them had really understood what it was all about and she just assumed she was a Christian. She attended church at Christmas and occasionally Easter, and she just shot up a prayer whenever she had a problem. People talked about so called born-again Christians in a disparaging way and called them holy-rollers and hypocrites. She certainly didn't want to be one of them and yet she knew in her heart something was missing. Maybe she could pick up a bible and some other books to find out more about her own faith and that of different religions in the world. It might be interesting to compare them and see what different religions believed in.

She found one written by a Professor of Psychology who lived in a village in the Cotswolds. It was called 'More Lives than One' and was the story of his interviews with numerous people about past lives they appeared to have had. It was very compelling when he took them back under hypnosis. Some had even spoken in foreign languages they had never learned. One person talked about herself being Jewish and the Jews being massacred after they had hidden in the Crypt of a Christian Cathedral. There was no evidence of such a place until it was discovered many years later and long after the book had been written. She knew Christians believed in eternal life if you followed Jesus, but this was a very different concept of being born back into this life again. She also read about Buddhism. They also believed in reincarnation, but it depended on what sort of life you had lived on earth. You could come back at a higher level or lower level according to the good or bad Karma you had created during your lifetime. She didn't like the idea of coming back as another person, or something else. She decided she would stick to Christianity, but she knew she had to dig much farther into it to find what she was looking for.

CHAPTER 46

Lawrence was doing some business trips to Europe and asked Jean to go with him to meet various clients. They had found an older lady who the children called Auntie Dorothy and she was able to stay with the children while she went. They had some day trips where they were able to go in the Company plane to places like Ghent in Belgium. While Lawrence was in his meetings the wives would take her on a tour of the various cities showing her many of the ancient sites and telling her about their history.

A meeting was planned for three days at a beautiful hotel called the Villa D'Este overlooking Lake Como in Italy. This was to entertain some of their most important clients after having record sales. The hotel was originally built as a Palace during the 16th century and was extremely luxurious in every aspect. It had an old world charm with all the advantages of modern facilities perfectly molded together. They took their clients on a boat trip around the lake with stunning views of the Alps, the small villages, and churches tucked into the hillsides. The big dinner event was to be held in the evening and everyone retired to their rooms to regroup later. Jean's head started to throb. "Oh no... I hope this isn't going to turn into a migraine," she told Lawrence. She had been suffering a lot with debilitating migraine headaches in recent times which completely knocked her out for two days and the pain was excruciating. Taking some pills she they laid down and prayed that it would disappear, but it just got worse. "I'm not going to manage the dinner tonight...I'm so sorry," Jean said. Lawrence patted her gently and told her not to worry he would bring her something to eat after the dinner.

He came back a few hours later with a sandwich and told her to try and eat something. Then he had to go back out again to say a final goodnight to his guests. She took a small bite of the sandwich just as he stepped back out of the door and as she tried to swallow, but it stuck in her throat and over her windpipe. She was choking and couldn't breathe. Panic stricken she waved her arms helplessly in the air and for some unknown reason Lawrence put his head back round the door and saw what was happening. Rushing over to her he bent her over and pushed her up and down. This was a rugby technique they used on the field when someone was winded. The sandwich flew out of her mouth. Making desperate wheezing noises she tried to get her breath back as he held her and gradually she was able to breathe again. It was a terrifying experience, but if he hadn't glanced back at her one more time it would have been a very different story. He had saved her life.

CHAPTER 47

Back home again Julie was getting ready to move to the local high School and Sally was leaving the private Catholic school to go into the regular school system. She had decided she was going to become a Nun after she felt that she had heard a voice telling her that it was God's plan for her. They weren't too sure about that, and she changed her mind very quickly when she started to notice boys. Jamie aged 7 had taken exams to get into Birkenhead School which was considered the best school in the area and he was doing really well. He was involved in cricket and other games and showed signs of becoming a very good athlete.

Julie managed to persuade Lawrence to come to their end of term sports and run in the Father's race. After so much travelling he was very unfit, but managed to win by turning back at the winning post and telling the other fathers they had to double back to the starting point. He had a head start and they all followed blindly but embarrassed the family by running off the field and throwing up. "Serves you right," Jean said, "that could have been called cheating." Nevertheless, Julie was really proud of her Dad.

Their lives were all busy. They added another Labrador called Katy which meant that there were now two dogs who were always getting into trouble. When Katy was still a puppy Jamie and his best friend, who he called Jamie Robrob, were in the garden playing with her. When they came in for tea Jean asked them where the puppy was. They looked at each other sheepishly. Eventually they owned up, they had put her in the dustbin because she was spoiling their game and forgotten to get her out again. She was non the worse for it, but they really had a good telling off.

They were mischievous little boys and had to be watched carefully especially as Jamie Robrob had Type 1 juvenile diabetes. His mother Lisa was Jean's best friend and trusted her to take good care of him. They were able to take him on vacation with them to their cottage at the beach, and Lisa showed Jean how to give him his insulin injections as well as an emergency shot in case he had a problem. Jean and Lawrence went out to dinner one night leaving the boys with a baby sitter. The next morning Jamie came into their bedroom early and said "Jamie Robrob is acting funny." Jean leapt out of bed and ran to their room realizing immediately that he was having a sugar high reaction, shaking, and feeling very thirsty. She immediately gave him the emergency shot which gradually settled him down. She was horrified, how could this have happened on her watch? The boys were very quiet and looking guilty. "What happened last night," she said. Hanging their heads they admitted that they had got into the biscuit tin while the baby sitter was watching the television and eaten all the biscuits and some chocolate that had been hidden away. Once again they were firmly chastised, but Jean was so relieved that Jamie Robrob was alright that they didn't give them any further punishment.

Lawrence's Chinese friend and also a business associate spoke to him about their daughter Alice. Jean had become friends with them too and had enjoyed the company of his wife when they were in Hong Kong. He said they wanted Alice to have a good education in England and planned to send her to boarding school. "Would you consider having her live with you during the school holidays?" he asked. They discussed it at length asking the children how they would feel about having Alice as a part of their family. They were all very happy about it although Jamie said he wasn't keen on having another potential sister. Two were more than enough for him. "Well she will be at school most of the time and the rest of the time we will look after her and treat her as one of our family," Jean said. Jean was able to take Alice to her new school and felt that it was so hard for her. She was not only moving to a new country but going to a new a boarding school and would not going to be able to see her family for a long time. It brought back memories of when she had first started boarding school when she was only 8 years old. She had sobbed for three days until she finally ran out of tears and finally began to accept what had happened to her. Alice of course was older but it would still be a very difficult transition for her.

CHAPTER 48

Lawrence was made President of the Liverpool Cotton Association which was the World's Arbitration Centre for settling major problems between Cotton Companies. It was a huge honour, but also a major responsibility and would mean even more travelling worldwide with his team to arbitrate disputes. His first visit was to be Poland and he would be going to many other countries as well as conducting business for his own company. Jean was being kept busy with the family, but decided that she needed to take some classes. She had always loved to paint and draw when she was young and had taken classes with an African Professor at Makerere College in Kampala. He had inspired her and taught her to capture the images of the African culture, the brilliant colours of the landscape, and beauty of the African people. She remembered how much she had felt what she called the rhythm of Africa with their dancing and music. She found a good teacher who could teach her, but it was very different and she really wanted to paint black faces rather than white.

Her teacher's husband was a sculptor and she felt very drawn to what he was doing but she knew she had limited time when she had a family to look after. She also needed to be available for Lawrence when he needed her to attend Conventions and help with business guests. He was invited to a luncheon of IFCATI, the World Textile Association which was being hosted in London with Prince Charles as the Speaker.

"Would you like to come?" he asked Jean.

"I would love to" she said, "maybe we'll get to meet him." They did but just to be introduced and all the conversation, of course, was all about textiles.

At the end of his year as President of the Liverpool Cotton Association they held their annual dinner at the Adelphi Hotel in Liverpool. Lawrence's company invited 80 guests flying them in from all over the world. Hotel accommodations had to be booked and arrangements of flowers and champagne were to be put into each room. Jean joined with his Secretary to welcome them on their arrival and to check them off on the list. She was also involved in booking some tours for the wives. Running around in jeans and shepherding them to their various locations. They were really surprised when she turned up in the evening with Lawrence. They had no idea that she was his wife they thought she was one of the staff. At the end of all the events a British Airways Trident jet was chartered to deliver their clients either to London to catch connecting flights on to Munich where others had connections to different European cities. It was an amazing experience to be in a private chartered plane and they could move around freely other than when they were landing or taking off. Lots of champagne was served and everyone was really chatty and enjoying themselves. Lawrence asked the pilot if some of them could go into the cockpit and see the pilot flying the plane.

"Just two at a time," he said.

Lawrence went up with his top German client and said to him, "Have you ever flown your own plane Karl?"

"Yes," he said. "I flew with the elite German Luftwaffe during the war. The planes were no match for the British Spitfires and out of 800 pilots only 4 of us survived." Lawrence changed the subject quickly. It would not be a good idea to tell him that the German bombers had been dropping bombs on him when he was a child.

After dropping off their remaining clients in Munich, they departed for Vienna, where they had planned a quiet weekend with Lawrence's business partner and his wife. They had booked a Penthouse Suite at the Hilton and when they walked in they couldn't believe their eyes. It was huge.... A 4,000 square foot suite at the top of the hotel. It was furnished with magnificent antique furniture and had a large sitting rooms, 2 bedrooms, 2 bathrooms, and a dining room. Beautiful paintings hung on the walls and other antique art pieces were placed in all the rooms. It was the epitome of charm, grace and luxury. They were told that Richard Burton and Elizabeth Taylor had stayed there several times.

Their weekend was relaxed and they felt ready to go on to their next Convention which was for the American Shippers in San Francisco. "We have a few days to spare before the meeting," Lawrence said. "I have booked us into the Lodge at Pebble Beach in Carmel for a weekend, but it also might be fun to go via Las Vegas for a couple of nights. We've heard so much about it and they have some very good shows," Jean jumped at the idea this was turning out to be a lot of fun for both of them.

Arriving at Las Vegas Airport they took a taxi to their hotel in the evening. The glitter of lights everywhere and the flashing neon signs were quite dazzling. They were met at the door of the hotel by porters who took their bags and they signed in at the reception desk. The porter waited to be tipped but their bags were handed to several more porters as they walked through the very long lobby and each one wanted to be tipped. "You have a beautiful suite," the final porter said as they walked into the room. It was all a garish green colour with pseudo French antique plastic chairs and tables and an enormous bed in the middle of the floor. Mirrors were all over the walls and when they collapsed on the bed there was one directly above them on the ceiling. It was so ugly compared to what they had come from in Vienna. They decided to leave as soon as they could, but would go to a show that evening. They enjoyed a nice dinner and the show started with the girls all in pink with feathered headdresses dancing and carrying large feather fans which were moved to cover their bare breasts. Suddenly just above them a group of three of the bare breasted dancers were lowered down from the ceiling right in front of them. They waved to the crowd who cheered loudly. Jean giggled and looked at Lawrence.

"What?" he said.

"You should have seen the look on your face," she said. "I swear if you hadn't got your glasses on your eyes would have popped right out." They both laughed and enjoyed the rest of the evening.

Arriving at Pebble Beach the following day they were once again treated to a gracious setting. Their room had beautiful views of the sea and rocky coastline overlooking the 18th Tee of the golf course. Lawrence couldn't wait to get his golf clubs out. "We'll definitely be coming back here again," he said. They drove to San Francisco after the weekend and met with many cotton friends at the Convention. There were business meetings and speeches by him, while Jean and some of the wives were able to explore San Fransisco. There was so much to see: the Golden Gate Bridge, Fisherman's Wharf, China Town and so many other fascinating places. It was a most exciting city and she loved it. In the evening there were special dinner parties for all the guests who had come from so many different countries, and on the last evening there was even a show featuring Tony Bennett. He sang 'I Left my Heart in San Francisco' which was a perfect end to an incredible trip.

All was well at home on their return, and the children welcomed them back effusively. "We've baked a special cake for you," the girls said. Between all of them they had decorated the house with balloons and welcome home signs that they had made. It was so special and it felt so good to be home again.

CHAPTER 49

Dawstone House

Lawrence was soon on the road, or rather, in the air again. He had purchased a Cotton Compress for the Company in Fresno, California which would necessitate him going there once a month. "I really enjoy the U.S.A." he said, "maybe we can move there one day, there are so many opportunities for future business and I like the American way of life. I find the people so welcoming."

"Definitely not," Jean said. "The children are all settled in schools here and our way of life is just fine. We have lots of friends and family nearby. We have already lived halfway around the world and finally feel happily settled here"

"I guess so. But never say never, why don't I take you all to Disneyland for Christmas this year it would be fun for all of us."

"Clever move," she thought, but she certainly wasn't going to turn that down.

One Sunday morning as he was reading the local paper after breakfast he glanced up and looked at her.

"Look at this," Lawrence said. "It is a house that has just come on the market. It is overlooking the River Dee with views of the Welsh hills. It is in two and a half acres has two tennis courts, one is a hard court, and the other a grass court as well as a swimming pool. It has large living areas and 7 bedrooms and 5 bathrooms. I think we should go and take a look at it."

Jean jumped at the idea. This surely indicated he wasn't really serious about moving to the States. They called a friend who was an Estate Agent and he made an appointment for them to go to see it that week. They were blown away. It had everything they could ever dream of in it. The views were magnificent, and they all fell in love with it.

"Can we afford it?" Jean asked.

"Yes," he said. "We will put our house up for sale and also the piece of land attached to it so we will be able to afford it."

The house was called Dawstone, and it had originally been built in 1894 as a Farmhouse and had been added to over the years. It would mean that the girls, including Alice, would all be able to have their own bedrooms. This would help with the sisterly fights they had from time to time. Jamie could have his own room too, and there was a huge cellar which they could turn into a games room for them. The cellar was part of the original structure and had rocky sandstone walls which made it feel old and mysterious.

"Do you think there might be ghosts down there?" Jamie asked. His sisters immediately started to go "Whooo Whooo," making ghostly noises

"Enough," Lawrence said, "there are no such things as ghosts stop trying to scare him." There was an opening at the bottom of the wall which was large enough for someone to crawl into. The opening appeared to be a passage, but they would have to block that off so that no one could explore it and get stuck. The main rooms were large and had huge windows looking out over the river, it was perfect. The owners were anxious to sell and pleased a young family were going to buy it, and so 2 months later the sale went through. They became the proud owners of their new home.

During the next few months Jean set about remodeling parts of the house. They needed new furniture, curtains, and the large kitchen needed to be upgraded. She wanted it to be a warm and welcoming place where they could all gather and have tea when the children came home from school. They turned the grass court into a lovely grassy area in front of the house and surrounded it with rose bushes, and decided to take out the swimming pool because of the amount of work it needed. The English weather was not ideal for a pool as the few weeks of summer there was far too much rain. Another pond would replace the pool and hopefully the two dogs they now had would not repeat the disastrous event they had in their old house. There were lots of shrubs and trees, and they wanted to leave most of the land more natural. Jean was delighted when bluebells appeared underneath the trees carpeting the ground with a vivid blue in contrast to the different shades of green that seemed to dance on the trees above. There was always a breeze, on the hillside and close to the river which varied from gentle to wild when storms came in.

Jean invited her friends to play tennis every week which was fun for all of them. Wandering around the garden amongst the trees one day she stopped at a small grassy knoll. It was about 30 feet high and covered in grass and weeds. She pulled some dead dry branches off the side of it and some of the grass came away. To her surprise she saw what looked like some rock underneath. She pulled a bit more grass away and saw that the rock appeared to be hand hewn and not just a natural outcrop. Excited she told the children that when they were off school at the weekend she wanted them to go with her to try and get more grass off it. They all went with every gardening tool they had and worked the whole day. Vines had wrapped themselves around underneath the grass. It was no easy task, but they could see there was some sort of a building underneath. A small Gothic shaped door started to appear and as they raked around the edges. The fully exposing it, they all put their weight on it to try and pry it open. They pushed and pushed and eventually broke through and the door opened up into what appeared to be a small Chapel. Covered in cobwebs the mark of a large cross stood above a

131

simple altar. Jean gasped, "My goodness…this must be a Chapel maybe going back to the 17th Century when the persecution of the Catholics took place during the reign of Henry the Eighth. They probably had secret services here and maybe the tunnel in our cellar could be a way they escaped. It would lead down to the river where they could get on a boat and cross the river to Ireland." Thoughts swirled around in her head as she pictured what might have happened in this place centuries ago. Vowing to dig into historical library books on the whole area she decided to try and find out what had happened in this old house and on its' grounds. She knew there must be a story and was determined to track it down once she had finished getting the house in order.

CHAPTER 50

F amily surrounded them for the first time in their life. Jean's parents had moved back to England from Africa and bought a house nearby. Lawrence's mother, sister, and brother Jim were fairly close to them too. They all really enjoyed family get togethers, especially at Christmas when Jean's brother, David, and wife Hilary were able to join them too.

The children loved to visit both Grandmothers and it was always eventful. Once when Jamie stayed overnight with Jean's parents he wandered outside and tried to open the gate which was locked. The gate was wooden and had fairly narrow slats in it. He put his head through one and got it firmly stuck. Florence was in the kitchen baking and didn't realize he had gone out. A neighbour happened to come along the street and got her husband to bring a saw to cut through the wood and get him out. He was sobbing and made them all laugh when he got home and told the story. "I thought they were going to cut off my head," he said.

He also made them laugh when they took him out to dinner to a special restaurant aged 7. He studied the menu very seriously and asked "What are these creeps?" They told him they were called crepes, a delicious French dessert, but of course his sisters fell apart giggling. The girls always enjoyed visiting their other Grandma too. Together, they would bake wonderful cakes and treats and they would dress up in their Aunt's jewelry. It was so nice to have family so near and they were always creating lots of memories. Jean had never felt so settled and happy. The house was almost finished and she could pursue some of the interesting history about it.

CHAPTER 51

"Can you get the children organized to stay with one of the Grandmas tonight?" Lawrence was calling from the office during the day which was not normal. "I want to have a talk with you on your own." Jean was puzzled, this was serious. Was it something to do with work?

She sent the children off for an overnight stay with their grandparents. She cooked a special meal, set the table, opened a bottle of wine, and waited for him to come home. He looked grim when he came in, and she wondered if he might have been fired.

"You are not going to be happy about this," he said, "but I have made the decision we need to move to the States." She looked at him in total horror and disbelief.

"We can't do this," she said. "We've moved into this beautiful home, the children are all settled in their schools, we have family and friends nearby. I just can't believe that you're thinking of moving us all over there." Tears started to fill her eyes.

"It's complicated, but I really believe the future of our business lies over there. We have to make the move. We will keep the house and possibly move back here in 5 years, but for now this is what we have to do. We will ask your parents if they would be willing to move into the house and take care of it and look after the dogs for us."

Jean burst into tears. She felt they had made their final move back to England, and for the first time in her life she felt completely settled.

"There is one other thing," he said. "I went ahead and bought a house on a golf course in Fresno. I didn't want to do this without you seeing it first, but I know you'll like it. You have started learning how to play golf here, so it will be a great opportunity for you to take it up more seriously."

She tried to process this as he spoke, it was all overwhelming, but she knew there would be no turning back. The decision was made, and they would be leaving for America in three months.

PART V

A Light on the Path- Faith and Miracles

CHAPTER 52

Leaving for America they all felt sad but also excited. Everyone seemed to think California was the ultimate place to live in. It was known for its' sunshine, gorgeous beaches, and way of life. Lawrence had wanted to make it special after uprooting them from their familiar lives, so they were booked to sail from Southampton on the Queen Elizabeth the 2ⁿᵈ (QE2) the newest Liner built by the Cunard Shipping Company. As the ship left the dock, they all hung over the rails watching England slowly disappearing, and a band played both English and American patriotic music. Flags were waved and balloons were released into the air. It was quite a send off as the ship gave two long farewell blasts on its horn. They were on their way across the Atlantic to New York. Their new life in America was about to begin.

The ship lived up to its reputation. It had every luxury on board; from the cabins, to the beautifully decorated lounges, dining rooms, and all the other facilities. There were flowers and champagne in their cabin and lots of activities for the whole family. The five days at sea passed by very quickly, and on the last day they all went out on the deck at dawn. As the ship moved towards the harbour in New York the Statue of Liberty appeared through the early morning mist. It was a truly special moment. As they all held hands and remembered how many people from all parts of the world had arrived in this country often fleeing from persecution in their own land. Some of their own ancestors may have even been on the first ship, the Mayflower, that sailed from England in 1620 carrying 102 men women and children to what was considered the New England.

As their ship docked they disembarked and were greeted warmly by friends of Jean's parents who lived in New York. Jud had been a pen pal friend of Jean's father when they were young boys in the Boy Scouts. They had kept in touch throughout their lives and had met only once when Ron and Florence had managed to visit them in America. Lawrence had bought them a ticket for their 40th wedding anniversary and they had a wonderful three weeks together travelling round much of the East coast. They had all sorts of plans too for Lawrence, Jean, and the family and took them on a tour around New York. They also took them to some great restaurants where they had the best Maine lobster they had ever had. They lived in a Brownstone house, which were townhouses made of sandstone that had been built in the early days of New York as it developed from a small town to the huge metropolis that it had now become. Jud was an advertising executive, and he and his wife took them to many of the historical sites and taught them so much about the history of America. On their final evening they took them to a Broadway Show and they left the next morning with such happy memories of time spent with this wonderful couple.

They flew into Denver and boarded the Zephyr train which would take them to Sacramento through beautiful countryside, passing through the Rocky Mountains, and stopping in Laramie and Cheyenne on the way. It all sounded very exciting until they found that the train was travelling through all these places during the night so they wouldn't get to see them. To add to this the restaurant car broke down, so Kentucky Fried Chicken was offered up to them at every stop. Lawrence did not like chicken so this was not the ideal journey they had hoped for.

"Let's think of some fun games," the girls said as they all sat cooped up in their small compartment with nothing to see out of the window.

"I know a good one," Jamie said, "let's play Poker!" They all looked at him in complete surprise.

"So what do you know about Poker? You are 10 years old and have never played the game. It is for grown-ups," Lawrence said.

Jamie grinned at his father, "Well I do know how to play it. Grandad taught me and I'll teach you if you like." They all laughed, especially at the look on their father's face.

Arriving in Sacramento they hired a car and drove to Fresno. They had to move into The Piccadilly Inn for the next 2 weeks. It was a difficult time- trying to get Sally and Jamie registered for schools, learning how to drive on the opposite side of the road, and trying to navigate the configuration of the roads in Fresno. Jean ended up more than once out in the country, but somehow managed to find her way back. It was all so different. They couldn't wait to see the house but when Lawrence had bought it he had rented it back to the owner and she was not moving out until the end of their second week there. Jean had to get a new Driving Licence. She took the test and failed, not once but twice. She couldn't believe it, she had been driving since she was 18. The examiner who was taking the test told her she drove too slowly the first time and too fast the second time. He was far from helpful. The third time she had a different examiner who passed her with no problem.

At last it was time to move into the house. Their furniture and household things had arrived and the house was now open for them to move into. It was situated on the golf course with lovely views over a lake. The sitting room was enormous with a large adobe fireplace at one end and huge windows from floor to ceiling. It was a stunning room and so different to the houses in England. The Architect was Cliff May, and this was one of his signature houses. They were all excited to find they had a swimming pool as well as a jacuzzi. Lawrence had bought them another beautiful home.

Julie had graduated from high school in England and had decided that she wanted to go to the world renowned Winkfield Cordon Bleu Cookery College in London which was owned by two famous ladies, Constance Spry and Rosemary Hume. Students studied there from all over the world due to the high reputation these women had and the

141

exceptional training that was given at their school. When Lawrence and Jean took her there to see the school they were really impressed. The buildings, the kitchens, and gardens were beautiful. They even grew all their own flowers, vegetables, and herbs which were used in their classes. Some of the students demonstrated their cookery skills and they were all treated to an outstanding lunch. Julie couldn't wait to get there and learn the secrets of cordon bleu cookery. She flew back to London after they had moved into the house. Sadly, even the swimming pool, jacuzzi, and life in the sun couldn't persuade her to stay.

CHAPTER 53

The schools had opened up in Fresno again after the long summer vacation, and Sally was able to start at Bullard High School which was located near by. After taking a test to find out her academic level they found she was a year ahead of her age group, so they wanted her to go straight into high school instead of junior high. As they drove into the car park on her first day it was full of very expensive looking cars. "Wow," Jean said to Sally, "They must pay the teachers really well over here for them to have these kind of cars." They soon found out that the cars actually belonged to the students, not the teachers. Jamie went to Forkner Elementary School which was very close by. When he came home after his first day, he said he didn't want to be called Jamie any more. "Why on earth not?" Jean said. "You have always been called Jamie."

"There's a girl in my class called Jamie and I don't want to have a girl's name," he said indignantly. From then on he became James, but it took them all awhile to get used to it.

Lawrence found some suitable offices and set to work getting a team together for this new part of their business which revolved around the Cotton Compress they had bought four years prior. He had initiated the move to improve the business and to become a part of the American cotton market. Another top Executive came with him from Liverpool as well as two younger Englishmen. The rest of the team were American employees who were already working at the Compress. They already knew some of the Cotton people who had other Companies and they gradually started to make friends and settled in to their new life. He quickly got involved with groups like the Western Cotton Shippers and would take Jean with him to some of the conventions and other business and social meetings.

Jean started to play golf and became quite competitive joining in some club tournaments. She really enjoyed it, but after the golf a lot of the ladies would stay on for lunch and some would continue for the rest of the day and play Bridge.

"Why do you always have to rush off home and not at least stay for lunch?" one of them asked.

"Well my husband comes home for lunch," Jean said.

"Can't he make himself a sandwich?" the woman said. Jean said no, but the truth of the matter was that with his work hours dealing with countries in different time zones he would go into work very early in the morning, come home for lunch and a swim, and then go back later in the afternoon for several hours communicating with the Far East. The lunch hour was special for both of them as they could actually spend some quiet time catching up with each other. Although he was still very much involved in international business he was able to trade more by telephone and concentrate on growing business in the American Cotton Market.

Fresno seemed to have so much to offer; classical concerts, a really good Museum, art galleries, shopping malls, and so many other interesting places to explore. The famed Yosemite National Park in the Sierra Nevada Mountains was only an hour away and the ocean and beaches were all within a similar range of distance. Fresno sat in California's Central San Joaquin Valley and was considered the breadbasket of the world. The huge farms grew every kind of fruit, nuts, and vegetables as well as large dairy farms which produced both beef milk and cheeses. 1.7 million acres of cotton were grown and picked by mechanical cotton-picking machines. When the crop was ready to be harvested vast areas of cotton stretched out across the landscape turning the countryside white as far as the eye could see.

CHAPTER 54

James on Soccer Team

As a family they began to find their way around, but it was a very different way of life and each of them struggled initially with the changes. Going into high school where everyone already had their group of friends was difficult for Sally. A lot of the girls there had long blonde hair and perfect figures, and she had short brown hair and a slightly rounder figure. Determined to look like the others she started on a serious diet, grew her hair long and dyed it blond. She needed a car and so Lawrence bought her an old Ram Charger which gave her some status as she was able to take some of the other girls out once she got her license. She eventually made some friends, but it took time. James joined the soccer team and although he was a good little player he had a problem with his knee and had to have surgery. Everyone at school was interested in his British accent and tried to copy him. When a vote at school was taken for the various student government positions he was voted in as Sergeant-at-Arms. He felt very pleased until he realized that he had to make a speech in front of the whole class. The morning of the speech he was very quiet at breakfast. Jean put his boiled egg and toast in front of him and said, "Are you feeling alright you haven't said a word?"

He shook his head and held his throat and he said in a husky whisper, "I've lost my voice." She immediately bent over to give him a hug and knocked his egg onto the floor. "You've broken my egg!" he said in a very loud voice. His sore throat plan had failed and he admitted he was scared of making the speech, and hoped he wouldn't have to go to school. They talked it through and Jean encouraged him. He ended up making a very good speech. He soon made a good friend called Paul whose family took them all under their wing and invited them to their very first Thanksgiving. It was very special to get to know this lovely family.

CHAPTER 55

Jean was exploring different things and when she visited the Museum she noticed there were sculpture classes available, and she signed up immediately. The clay and sculpture tools would be provided for the class and they could purchase these if they decided to continue with sculpting after their first lesson. There were 10 of them in the class and they had a nude male model. The teacher was excellent and demonstrated the figure of this young man explaining how the different muscles and body parts worked together. He said that this was the underpinning foundation of every good sculpture and that clothes could not be put on a figure until this had been worked on first. The class faithfully followed his instructions and as he moved them round to inspect the anatomy of the upper front of the thighs of this man they all glanced up at each other and tried to be serious as they all found themselves looking directly at his normally covered private parts. However, nobody said a word, after all this was art and the young model was completely unphased. They were able to take their sculpture home between classes and as the work progressed Jean's family began to tease her. "He looks really good," they said, "but he doesn't have his you-know-what, when are you going to finish it?" They all laughed and she finally put a big blob of clay on the pelvic region just to please them.

Her first sculpture was complete and she knew that the moment she'd put her hands in the clay that it would be the beginning of something very special that she wanted to pursue. She took more classes advancing her knowledge of anatomy as she started to make figurative art. She loved the creative process and felt at times it had a life of its own and brought out some unexpected results. Her first sculptures were all of black people, because she found it hard to sculpt a white person. Her years growing up in Africa had obviously deeply impacted her. She still carried the memories of that time in her heart and it was expressing itself in her work.

CHAPTER 56

Grandma and Grandad Black and Auntie Win

They were all gradually beginning to settle down, but in the back of their minds they were still hoping to be able to go back to England in five years. They were enjoying their Fresno life, but it felt as if they were just on a long vacation. They had several visitors from home during their first three months and it was a joy to take them to Yosemite National Park and to the ocean in Carmel. 'Don't know why you'd want to come back to England," several of them said, "this place is fantastic and on top of that you have so much sun. You know how England is so cold and rainy most of the time."

Jean nodded. "Well we are coming home to spend Christmas with the family," she said, "so I may have a change of heart once we get back into a cold English winter."

Jean's parents had moved into their house in England and were happy to take care of the two dogs. This also meant Julie had a home to go to after she moved back to England. Things seemed to be working out well for all of them.

"Remember that I told you what was happening with the business when we were on our way over here," Lawrence said, "and that there was talk of a merger with our Company Ralli Bros and Coney and Cargill who are the largest private Company in the world? It was all top secret and we had to keep it to ourselves while all the negotiations were going on."

"I do," Jean said, "but I didn't really take it in. There was so much going on at the time."

"Well it does appear that it might be going through. I have been asked to go to Minneapolis to meet with the Board of Directors and hopefully find out what will be happening."

He left the following day and was back a day later with news that once more she did not want to hear. "The merger has gone ahead and so we are now going to be a part of Cargill and as their cotton business is in Memphis they want to move us there. The office here will not be closed down, but they want me and our other top executive to be in their main office in Memphis."

Jean swallowed hard, she had got beyond crying at each bombshell and her mind flew into a flurry of different scenarios. She was not going to uproot them all again. "Well, maybe we could move back to England as we had already planned, or the children and I could stay in Fresno and you could commute home each weekend."

"Unfortunately, it doesn't work either way," he said. "Cargill has already merged their own team with Ralli Bros and Coney in Liverpool and no longer need me there and they want me to be a part of their team in Memphis."

"Well I don't intend to move there in a hurry," she said. "I will come over with you to meet the team and see what it looks like, but if we do have to move I will stay here until the end of the school year."

"My thought is," Lawrence said, sensing rebellion on his hands "…

is that we should send James back to boarding school in England so his education doesn't get completely mixed up. We hope to go back there eventually and he will have his grandparents nearby. Sally is a year ahead so I'm sure she would be able to fit in to a high school in Memphis depending on what the schools are like there of course."

Both Sally and James were not happy at the thought of moving again although the idea of going back to school in England appealed to James. He still missed his friends from there. Sally said she had no intention of moving as she had settled in at school and had acquired a boyfriend. A week later they flew to Memphis and met with the people that Lawrence would be working with. They showed them around the city and had even found a house that they wanted them to buy. It was a typical southern home surrounded by trees. They were taken out to dinners and to the home of the chief executive and although they were all very welcoming Jean had an overwhelming feeling that this was not going to be the right place for Lawrence to be. Something did not feel right, but she tried to put her feelings to the side knowing she didn't really want to move again. Memphis was hot, very humid, and felt claustrophobic. However, it looked like they had no choice and Lawrence decided to put a deposit down on the house. "I really don't have a good feeling about this move," Jean said. "The group are all very nice, but they seem to work in an entirely different way to you, and I'm not sure that you would find it easy to fit in with them."

Arriving home they started to put things into place for their next move and contacted Mostyn House, a boarding school in England, near to the grandparents for James. This was not an easy decision, but it seemed the right thing to do. He had only been out of the English school system for a short time and would probably be able to catch up quite quickly. Jean flew back with him and felt devastated when she had to leave him at the school. She remembered how hard it had been for her when she first went to boarding school. Her parents reassured her they would keep a close eye on him and take him out for some weekends. Lawrence was flying back and forth to Memphis for meetings and the plan was for them to move there in eight weeks. He decided to go ahead and complete the purchase of the Memphis house which meant they now had to sell the Fresno house. Sally would just have to move with them as she would no longer have a home there. It was all so difficult and it was the first time in their lives they didn't seem to have control over what was happening to them.

Lawrence asked her to go with him to Memphis again before their final move so she could get to know more about what to expect when they got there. After a few days she said, "I don't know how to say this, but everything in me tells me that we are making a big mistake. I don't believe that you will fit in there and be happy."

He gave her a long hard look and said, "I have always valued your opinion… so give me some time to think it over."

A few days later he said, "I have asked to take a four-month sabbatical. Everything has been happening so fast, and we probably do need more time to think this through." Jean gave a sigh of relief; however, she knew if he didn't take the job he would be out of work for the first time in his life which was frightening.

CHAPTER 57

News always moved around fast in the cotton market and it soon became known Lawrence was taking a sabbatical and not moving immediately to Memphis. A cotton broker called him soon after and said he knew that Continental Grain, the second largest grain company in the world, were thinking about moving into the cotton business. "Why don't you contact them? With your experience you could be just the person they are looking for."

Lawrence immediately got in touch with them and was asked to fly to New York to meet with them for an interview. They explained they wanted to start a cotton business and asked him to present a business plan for this new venture for them. Arriving home he immediately started working on a plan getting Jean to help in typing the paperwork. They both felt energized and excited at the thought of what this might mean if it was accepted. He flew back to New York to present the plan and they spent a few anxious days on his return waiting to hear the result.

The phone rang early one morning, "We find your business plan very interesting," said their Financial Director. "The owner of Continental Grain would like to meet with you to discuss it further. He is currently in St. Moritz in Switzerland having a Board meeting and would like to have you and your wife fly over there as soon as possible."

Lawrence set the phone down and called Jean immediately. "They really must be interested if they want to fly us out to St. Moritz. How soon can you be ready?"

"Right now," she said, "who wouldn't be excited to fly to St. Moritz.

I'm really thrilled and this could be a new start where we could stay in Fresno." Continental Grain booked flights and hotel accommodations for them and they left for Zurich via Heathrow the next day. They were also booked by train for the journey into the Alps to St. Moritz. As they travelled through the delightful Swiss countryside with pretty picturesque villages and churches nestled on the mountainside, it almost felt surreal. It was as if they had been transported to an incredibly beautiful and serene landscape. The train moved through several tunnels and started to climb upward into the Alpine pastures and the snow covered mountains. Lawrence had asked a friend of his from England who was a Financial Advisor to join them and they spent most of the journey fine tuning his business plan for the meeting. They all moved into the Park Hotel on the night they arrived and after a delicious Swiss breakfast were able to relax during the day until their meeting which would take place at 5:00 p.m. at their hotel.

Lawrence was called in to meet the Board of Directors and after discussing his plan to open a new worldwide Cotton Company for them, based in Fresno in the USA, they asked him to return to New York again to work out a few more details. They had decided to accept his plan and welcomed him on board. The relief was huge. They were once again able to plan for their future and could stay in Fresno. They knew that Sally would be so happy and they could bring James home again to be with them. They had missed him so much and knew it had been hard for him in boarding school so far away. Gibson Elementary School which he would be coming back to sent an entry test for the Gifted And Talented Education (G.A.T.E.) program which he had to take. The G.A.T.E. program was an accelerated program designed for children who were above average. Whether he passed the test or not the plan was to bring him back to Fresno, but James had thought that coming back to Fresno depended on whether he passed the test or not and he was scared to death he might fail. After he heard the news he was coming home he wrote to them saying, "When you told me I was coming home I felt as if I'd died and was coming back to heaven," such profound words for an eleven year old. It was a very emotional moment for all of them.

CHAPTER 58

Once everything settled down again and Memphis had been informed they were not going to join Cargill, Lawrence got to work starting ContiCotton, their new Company. He found new offices, hired new people, and spent two months organizing his business plan. There was a lot to do. Starting a new business from scratch was very challenging, but he felt really energized and determined to give his very best to making this an excellent cotton company. He added offices in Lubbock, Texas and asked Jean to go with him to Hong Kong and Japan to appoint Sales Agents for their business there. Jean stayed in the hotel while he was out contacting various people and she was able to take phone calls and notes for him as well as meeting many of the people he would be involved with. It was a very hectic and interesting time, and they were both excited at this new direction their lives had taken.

Things were going well at home too and they were all so thankful to be staying in Fresno. With Lawrence working long hours and the children at school, Jean decided to progress her interest in sculpture and signed up at Fresno State University to take classes on mold making and bronze casting. This was a fascinating process which involved making a reinforced mold to create a replica of the sculpture. After removing the mold from the sculpture, liquid wax was then poured into it and allowed to harden. The wax was then melted out in a kiln leaving an imprint of the sculpture inside the mold. It was an ancient method called the lost wax process which was first used by people 6,000 years ago to cast small amulets. Finally the liquid bronze was poured into the mold at 1,150 centigrade and left to harden. The bronze sculpture had to be broken out of the mold and when Jean found herself on top of a dumpster one day using all her strength to break open a mold with a hammer she seriously began to wonder what on earth she was doing. It was all worth it though, and after the final stages of using acids and a blow torch to put colour on the finished piece she felt a sense of achievement in what was turning into her new career. This also would fit in with Lawrence needing her to go to conventions, meetings, and being available for the children as she could be working from home. She gave up golf and took up tennis which took a lot less time and she started producing sculptures which was something she always wanted to do. Sally had been growing up fast during this time and was able to help ferrying James back and forth from school when needed. He was doing well at Gibson Elementary School in the G.A.T.E program that both he and his friend Paul were in.

CHAPTER 59

The new business was making good progress and the company decided they wanted him to find a qualified American cotton person who was familiar with the Australian cotton market to open an office for them in Australia. He immediately thought of his friend Will who was already living in Moree in New South Wales, a town way out in the boonies as the Aussies would say. Will was available and in a very short time Lawrence and Jean were on their way to meet with him and his wife Carol. They arrived and stayed overnight in Sydney leaving the next morning on a small aircraft to Moree. When they were about to board the aircraft an announcement was made that the plane was overbooked and they would have to bump some people and put them on the evening flight. Only one of them could get on the flight and as Lawrence had important meetings as soon as he arrived there he would have to go and leave Jean behind. She wasn't unduly worried as she had an Australian girlfriend who was living in Manley a ferry ride across the bay.

Her friend was thrilled to hear from her and told her to jump on the Ferry and spend the day with them. They would take her back in the evening to catch her flight. "Moree… why on earth would you be going there it's way out in the bush and where a lot of Aboriginies live," her friend said. They had a fun day together and Jean was back in good time to catch the plane. They finally arrived in Moree at 10:00 p.m. in the evening, after two stops on the way. Everyone piled off the plane, but there was no sign of Lawrence or Will and they were starting to close up the airport for the night. Jean approached the only couple left and explained her predicament, but it was worrying as she had no phone number or address.

"Who are the people you are visiting?" the woman said. "Moree is so small we know everybody." When Jean told her who they were visiting the woman said, "No problem, we have a small open top car, so it will be a bit of a crush, but we will take you there." Jean sat with her case on her lap in the back of their open top car feeling so relieved. It was very dark outside, there were no lights in sight. Looking up at a black velvety sky studded with stars that almost felt close enough to touch she saw two shooting stars, surely that was a good omen. Here she was in the middle of Australia with two complete strangers going goodness knows where.

Finally, some lights came into view as the couple cheerily said, "Here we are, just walk up the driveway and knock on the door," as they dropped her off. Nervously she walked up to the door and knocked. A large dog suddenly appeared barking furiously at her she was terrified, it sounded as if it was going to attack her and no one was answering the door. Looking around she saw what appeared to be another house nearby so lugging her suitcase behind her she gingerly made her escape from the barking dog. This was a nightmare. It was now almost midnight and would anybody answer the door at this time of night? Approaching the house there was no sign of a dog this time and someone came to the door when she knocked. As soon as she told them what had happened they said, "Oh you poor thing, come on in and we'll give you a cup of tea or something stronger. We'll call Will and give those men an Aussie mouthful in words you probably won't want to hear."

Will and Lawrence soon turned up full of apologies saying they had been so involved in their meetings they had forgotten to pick her up. Jean glared at them stony-faced, but left it to her new friends to tell them off...she was beyond words.

After such a bad start things soon turned around when she met Carol, Will's lovely wife, and their little 3 year old girl called Molly. Carol gave her such an insight into what it was like to live in such a rural area in Australia. Moree was a very small place and neighbours all helped each other. She and Will gave a barbecue party for them and Carol told her the history of the Aborigine people who were the very first known inhabitants of the country. They lived about 20,000 years ago and were deeply connected to the land for their physical and spiritual needs and were illiterate. They passed on their stories through painting on rocks. When discovered by Captain Cook in the 1700's he claimed the country for the British Crown and sadly because of the diseases the sailors brought with them large numbers of Aborigines died. Knowing how interested Jean was in art Carol took her to see a local Aboriginal artist. She was fascinated by the dots creating circles which really spoke to her of their connection to the land and the universe they lived in. Inside the caves where they lived were paintings of hands and animals on the walls which were all part of their ancient story.

Will was the perfect fit for the new Company and knew many cotton people and the way things worked in Australia. Lawrence had booked them flights to go on to the east coast of Australia for a few days to visit the Great Barrier Reef. They went on a small boat and were able to swim and see the incredible beauty of the coral reef. The ship took them to a small island one evening at sunset and as they waded onto the shore they were told to stay in while they threw fish food into the water. Brightly coloured fish suddenly swarmed around their legs which were lovely to look at, but felt a bit creepy. Jean hoped sharks wouldn't decide to come in and make a meal of them. They were able to go to a butterfly center where they saw huge blue butterflies that were living in the rain forest. They went on a ride over the canopy of the rain forest which was stunning and even had dinner in a marquee which was set up inside the forest. Unfortunately, there was a thunderstorm and torrential rain, and they had to walk out in the dark and mud to find their way back to the bus that was waiting for them.

CHAPTER 60

Back home Sally and James were doing well. They had aquired a cocker spaniel puppy named Toby before they had left and a homeless kitten had been added to the family called Jemima. Their next door neighbour not realizing they had been away said, "It sounded like you had a great party a week ago." Sally and James had to own up as they had been told, "No parties while we are away." They both had friends at the party and James had what they called his Charles Street Gang who were all his buddies from school. No harm done except for some very loud music.

They planned to go back to England for Christmas and had a wonderful time with Julie, Jean's parents, her brother David and wife Hilary and their sons, Lawrence's sister Win and brother Jim, plus other family members which made it a real family gathering. They celebrated a true English Christmas with turkey, stuffing, and all the trimmings. The ceremonial plumb pudding soaked in brandy and lit with a flame was brought in at the end. Christmas crackers had been pulled and everyone was wearing their silly paper hats all at various angles after they had been drinking Lawrence's famous champagne and brandy cocktails. It was a Christmas to remember.

They made it a family tradition after that and planned to go back every Christmas, but surprisingly Jean didn't feel she wanted to go back to live there anymore. Fresno now felt very much like home. The weather was very cold and Jean asked her parents if they would like to come to Fresno each year and spend six months with them during the winter. They were delighted and so they decided that they would fly out and stay with them from October to March each year. Dawstone, the house they were looking after for them in England, had become too much for them to cope with any more. Lawrence said, "We'll sell it, and as much as we have enjoyed being in our house here in Fresno on the golf course I think we need to look for something different that maybe has a guest house. We have so many visitors who usually come for two weeks at a time and now with your parents coming for three months I think we need to have separate accommodation for them." Jean totally agreed, with the large windows and golfers continuously passing by on the course she felt a lack of privacy. She was always having to rescue Toby who would squeeze through the bars of the fence and chase the ducks and geese on the course... annoying the golfers.

They started to look at houses and before long found the ideal house which they totally fell in love with. As they walked through a large circular wrought iron gate towards the front door through a peaceful garden with a koi pond and waterfall she knew this would be the one. The house was set in an acre with a swimming pool and a lovely back garden. The rooms inside were all spacious and full of light with each room overlooking different parts of the garden even a cactus garden which was viewed from the kitchen. There was a guest house which was separated from the house by a walkway. A staircase outside led to a large room upstairs which would be perfect for James who had recently put together a band and the music was loud. There was a very large greenhouse at the back of the garden which had been used for growing orchids and Jean earmarked it immediately for an art studio. It was exactly what they wanted and before long they were able to move in and start to enjoy their new home.

CHAPTER 61

C ontiCotton was growing fast and the owner of Continental Grain decided to come and see for himself this new Company in California that he now owned. He and his wife flew in from New York on their private jet and Lawrence had arranged an itinerary to show them as much as possible during the few days they would be there. After meeting all the company employees and being taken to see the huge cotton fields and ginneries in the Valley he expressed a wish to visit the Yosemite National Park as well as the famous Pebble Beach Golf Course and resort in Carmel. Lawrence had booked rooms at the luxurious Lodge overlooking the ocean on the 18th hole. They were amazed at the magnificence of the Yosemite Valley and the spectacular views of the sheer granite cliffs towering. Bridal Veil waterfalls were 3,600 feet above the valley and the falls were cascading down surrounded by a fine mist which seemed to be ethereal and almost magical. They were really enjoying their visit to California, and Lawrence was really pleased with the way things were going. As they left to travel to Merced where their plane was parked they asked to sit in the back of the car where they could perhaps catch a quick nap after all their travels. Lawrence muttered quietly to Jean, "There's a car behind that keeps driving up far too close to us and now he seems to be fighting with a woman who is trying to get out of the car." In a few minutes the car was back behind them again and honking the horn. "Don't know what his problem is?" Lawrence said. "There's plenty of room to overtake." Suddenly the car pulled round them and came to a screeching halt a few feet away in front of them. Lawrence put on the brakes and stopped and a huge tall angry looking man with wild red hair and a beard stormed over towards them. Just as he reached the car Jean said, "Lock the doors!" He tried to open the door and then started beating and kicking on the car yelling obscenities. They were all in shock and Lawrence tried to slowly start pulling away from this vicious man and then took off as quickly as he could. He drove fast and left him way behind. They had no idea what it was all about, but it certainly wasn't a good ending to what had been a really enjoyable visit.

CHAPTER 62

Jean had been creating a lot of sculptures and continued to take sculpture classes. She had even flown to Taos with her friends Pauline and Arminee to study art with Rosalind Cook who was a renowned sculptor. Taos was an interesting place and she was fascinated by all the art shops that were so involved in the New Age culture. At home she had started showing her work in Galleries and was beginning to have some success with sales. A friend from England who had been to visit them offered to do an art show for her in her art gallery in England. Jean was able to send 25 bronze sculptures over for the show and invitations were sent out to some of their old friends as well as people who were listed in the gallery. On the night of the show she felt very nervous. Would she be able to sell anything? It had been an expensive venture getting all the sculptures there. People started to arrive and several friends had no idea she had been doing this in the States. They were surprised to see what she had done. A large crowd arrived and stood around viewing, talking, and having a glass of wine. Nothing much seemed to be happening although everyone seemed to be enjoying themselves. Suddenly a red dot was placed on one of the sculptures indicating that it had been sold and as if by magic other red dots started to appear. Her heart beat faster and she had a second glass of wine to calm her nerves. At the end of the evening she couldn't believe what had happened, 23 of her sculptures had been sold, it had been an amazing success.

Flying back home to Fresno she felt so thankful she had found something she truly loved to do and now she had her perfect studio in the peaceful garden of their new home. She started to give classes there and eventually was joined by several other artists who enjoyed the ambience of the creative spirit which inspired them all.

One of her students was a young girl of 12 who had been completely blind from birth. Holly was a bright and bubbly child who loved singing, writing, and telling stories. She had an incredibly positive attitude about her disability. In fact she ignored it and was prepared to tackle anything. She had a strong faith in Jesus and was not praying for him to restore her sight, but believed that He would always look after her. She was a true inspiration. She had never seen a face so Jean taught her to create a bust by feeling her own face and where the eyes, nose, ears, and mouth were set and she made two really good busts in clay which were fired in the kiln. She was a very special student and Jean felt so honoured to be able to teach her.

CHAPTER 63

Elephant

Lawrence wanted to take the family to Africa and was able to organize a trip during the school vacation. He wanted the children to see where Jean had grown up and where they had met and married. They invited James's friend Paul and his parents as well as Jean's parents and some friends from England to join them. In all they would be a party of 12. They planned to start out at Treetops the Game Lodge that was built in 1932 on stilts amongst the tree tops where Princess Elizabeth had become the Queen of England when she was given the news that her father King George had died. A guide picked them up at Nairobi Airport in a Minibus and took them on the three-hour drive to their first destination. They were all tired after their long journey and were thankful to have hot showers and dinner available on their arrival.

The rooms were very comfortable, but they knew that they might not get much sleep that night as they overlooked a large saltlick waterhole where the animals came in at night and they would see them at close range. The staff told them they would knock on their doors and wake them up when animals were outside. Just after midnight there was a loud rap on the door and they staggered out sleepily onto their balcony to a most amazing sight. Just below them and lit up by low lights were several elephants with their babies as well as a few buffalo and waterbuck foraging in the huge waterhole and salt lick. It felt almost surreal. They were so close that they could see all the details on them. Nobody spoke and they all watched them until the elephants gradually moved away.

The next day they left early after breakfast for their next destination to see the flamingoes on Lake Naivasha. As they approached the lake a large part of it appeared to be pink and it was covered by thousands of flamingoes noisily catching fish and strutting round with their ungainly looking necks on the beach. Their guide took them to a quieter area of the lake to get on a small boat and sail around the lake. It was very peaceful until they came very close to a pod of hippos who kept breaking up from the water, blowing hard, and grunting. The guide was not at all concerned and tried to get really close, far too close for comfort for them. He also spotted a leopard in a tree and drove the open topped Minibus right underneath it. The leopard woke from its sleepy state and started to climb down making them all nervous thinking how quickly it could suddenly jump right down on top of them.

The next day they left for the Maasai Mara to view Mount Kilimanjaro and to see the migration which took place every year. Tens of thousands of wildebeest and zebra have to cross the Mara River to get to the grassy plains for their food and the crocodiles have a feeding frenzy as they attack the helpless animals in the water. It was a day's drive away over dirt roads full of potholes and there had been some recent storms that were making them muddy. As they came round a bend a large truck was sitting in the middle of the road. It had broken down and was up to its axels in mud completely blocking the road. On each side of the road there were high grassy slopes and there was no way they could get past it. Their driver swore and turned to them and said, "We will have to go back and take a different route, but it will take us two more days to get to the Mara." Another Minibus appeared behind them with several other tourists and they all got out to try and find a solution. "I have it," someone said, "we have enough men here to try and push the buses up the slope and drive round at the top and get back onto the road." It was worth a try so the women got out while the men started to try to push the buses up. All the women from both buses were desperate for a bathroom at this stage and so helped each other up the slope and headed for the nearest bushes feeling very nervous. Just as they positioned themselves pants down the first bus shot over the top of the slope giving their African driver a bird's eye view of eight white bottoms all sticking out from behind the bushes. They were mortified, but no doubt the driver had a story or two to tell when he got home.

It was late afternoon when they arrived and Mount Kilimanjaro was covered in clouds, but the next morning it was crystal clear as it stood out on the vast green plains of the Maasai Mara which stretched as far as the eye could see. Zebra, wildebeest, buffalo, bushbuck, and other deer as well as the occasional giraffe, leopard and a pride of lions roamed freely grazing on the nutritious grass. There were no huge herds, the migration had only just started and these were the early arrivals who had successfully crossed the river. Their guide took them to a small Maasai village where they were welcomed and able to look around their smallholdings. The Maasai were brave warriors who came from an ethnic tribe who lived on the plains. The men were very tall usually between 6' and 7' in height and wore a red Shuka made of cow skin and they usually carried a spear to protect themselves against the wild animals. They lived off the land and had herds of cattle which provided them with milk, blood, and meat. They would drink the cows' blood mixed with milk and eat the meat which was sufficient nourishment for them. The women wore similar clothes, but with a lot more decoration as they were very adept at making beadwork. It was beautiful work and they sold bracelets and necklaces to the visitors. After touring the village and peeking into their small wooden huts they were asked to dance with them. They started to sing and clap and they all were caught up in the true African rhythm which Jean remembered so well.

The next day they drove to the Mara River and were amazed to see the thousands of animals trying to cross over, but it was also hard to see the ones that were caught and dragged away by the crocodiles. There were so many other sights and sounds including a lion kill, baboons clambering all over their van, and a very close call with an elephant in musth who came directly towards them on the road. "This is not good," the driver said. "He is ready to mate and intoxicated by lust. They are aggressive and likely to challenge anything that is likely to get in their way." He stopped the Minivan and they all held their breath as the elephant came closer and closer. Jean said back up to the driver, but he seemed to be mesmerized by this enormous bull elephant that was nearly on them. At the last minute, and only a few feet away, it trumpeted, flapped its ears, and turned off into the bush. There was a stunned silence as they all breathed a huge sigh of relief. This had been a really scary encounter.

On their final night they sat outside on the verandah of the Lodge where they had pre- dinner drinks and watched a glorious African sunset. The sky reflected the beauty of this land, the deep blue, red, and gold colours sweeping out across the vast savannah as the sun slowly descended beyond the horizon seeming to echo the mystery and vibrancy of its people. It stayed in your heart long after you had left.

CHAPTER 64

There was one thing left to do when they travelled back to Nairobi to catch the plane home. Jean wanted to take her parents to her old school, the Kenya High School for girls in Kileleshwa on the outskirts of Nairobi. They had never seen the school in all the time she had been there. They lived so far away in Uganda it was difficult for them to make the journey especially during the time of transition from British rule to self-government in Kenya. Jean felt a little nervous, this was now a school with nearly all black students with a black Headmistress and staff. How would she be received? Would they feel resentful that she had been a privileged white child during the time she was there?

The school looked much the same as it had been when they arrived and they were pointed to the Headmistresses office by some very helpful girls. Jean knocked tentatively on the door and a voice said, "Come in!" A large black lady was sitting behind her desk and glanced up at her. "What can I do for you?" she said.

"I wanted to come back and see the school again. I was a student here many years ago before Independence and I have brought my mother with me as she never had a chance to see it when I was here!" Jean blurted out. The Headmistress rose up from her chair and came round her desk and enveloped Jean in an enormous bear hug.

"Welcome back!" she said. "I'm so pleased you've come back to see us. Let me meet your family and I will order some tea for us all." Jean felt tears starting to well up in her eyes at the kind generosity of this lovely woman.

After tea she told them they were welcome to go all around the school and Jean took them on a tour reminiscing about all the years she had spent there. She even confessed to some of the mischief she and her friends had been up to during their time there.

CHAPTER 65

The next few months became increasingly busy as Lawrence was made President of the American Cotton Shippers Association which covered all the cotton merchants in the United States as well as setting their policies throughout the world. This was a great honour and during his year of office he would be travelling to many countries around the world for them as well as managing his own business, ContiCotton. A convention was held at the end of each year and all Association members, Presidents and Past Presidents, were invited to the four-day event which would be in different parts of the country. Hawaii was the venue for the outgoing President this year and Lawrence would be taking over very soon after that. They had both been to many of the former President's Conventions where they usually brought in interesting speakers such as the Secretary of Agriculture and Senators as well as Barbara Walters and Bob Hope, who of course was hilarious.

At the end of the meetings and after the final speeches and dinner, several of the heads of competing companies stayed on to play golf. Over time they had grown to know each other very well and had created their own Ryder Cup game with a Captain of the USA team and a Captain of the Rest of the World team. It was always fiercely competitive, but full of fun and so much camaraderie. Not many heads of competing businesses could have also become such good friends, the cotton business was truly unique in this respect.

One of Lawrence's ACSA meetings was held in Washington D.C. and an itinerary had been set up for the wives of the directors to visit the

White House and Blair House where honored guests from all over the world had stayed. Jean was excited at the prospect but was not prepared for the snowstorm that arrived just ahead of them. As their group was led into a long entryway outside where they were checked and asked to wait until it was their turn to go inside they stood in the snow and her feet in her lightweight shoes started to go numb. "Sorry folks," said the tour guide," It looks like it may be another hour before they let us in as it appears there has been some sort of incident." Stumbling into the White House an hour later she couldn't even feel her feet but somehow managed to get inside. They toured the magnificent blue, red, and green rooms in the East Wing as well as the State Dining Room and the China Room, finishing up with a view of the White House Rose Garden. So much history and so many Presidents had passed through these corridors, it was a truly momentous occasion to be able to set foot inside this famous building.

CHAPTER 66

After Julie had finished her two-year cookery course in England they had asked her to stay on for a third year to teach incoming students. She had then decided to move back home to be with the family for a while. She found a job at the Piccadilly University Inn and moved into an apartment with a friend in Fresno. Sally had graduated from high school and after completing her first year at UC Davis she wanted to go back to England to be with a boyfriend she had known when she was growing up. Before long they got engaged and they all flew back for her wedding. It looked as if she would now live in England. James was at Bullard High School and had a lovely girlfriend who they liked very much called Jennifer. He said he and Jen were just good friends, but they thought that it may be a bit more serious than that. Jen was a part of their group and went to watch them play some of their gigs with their band Chum and the Frenzy. The band was very important to them and they spent endless hours practicing in his large upstairs room. Although it was so noisy Jean felt that it kept them out of trouble and she liked some of the lyrics they had written themselves. "The song I like the most, James" she said "is 'Good Body Babe…and I do a little jiggle to it when I hear it in the kitchen"

He gave her a big smile, "Wrong words Mum, that one is actually "Goodbye These Days". It became one of those family jokes for quite a while. They practiced at Paul's house one day when his parents were away. What they didn't know was that the room was next to a specially designed room where Paul's father kept his collection of very fine wines.

He was horrified when he found out that the loud music had popped the corks of these carefully preserved wines. He did realize though that they hadn't done this on purpose and very generously forgave them. They were all going to be moving on before long to various universities, James to UC Santa Barbara and Jen to Westmont, but they all planned to keep up their playing when they were home on vacation. James was also a keen golfer and Lawrence wanted to give him a chance to play on some of the major courses in Scotland, and so they decided to have a special Father-Son trip together. They booked tee times at St Andrews, Kings Barn, Carnoustie, Prestwick, Troon, and Turnberry. This would be a lot of golf in five days and Jean warned James not to wear his father out. Needless to say they took no notice and had an amazing time together.

CHAPTER 67

The empty nest syndrome had arrived and Jean found she had more time to follow some of her own interests. She could spend more time in her studio creating art and enjoyed doing some Art Show fundraisers for various charities. Working on her art was a very meditative and peaceful process which seemed to take her beyond her normal thoughts to a sense of spirituality and God. She was still searching for answers and surely He would give them to her. She joined the Church of Religious Science for a while and took courses on Christianity as well as other religions and the power of positive thinking. It seemed to her that all religions led to God except for Christian beliefs that there was only one way to heaven and that was by accepting Jesus Christ as the Saviour of the world who was sent to reconcile us to God and have our sins forgiven. She remembered once again about the Missionary who had preached at her Crusaders group when she was so young and how scared she and her friend Molly were when he told them they would go to hell if they didn't believe in Jesus. She still felt something was missing. She considered herself a Christian, but there were still many unanswered questions in her heart and mind.

What was she missing that made her feel that there was still much more? She had looked in so many different directions and prayed to God that He would lead her to a much deeper understanding and the way to the truth. Lawrence was getting concerned with what he called her "out-of-the-box-leanings" toward other religions. He had been brought up with a strong Baptist background and although he hadn't been attending church he didn't want her to get involved with these other faiths.

"I think we should join a church where we can both get into some Bible studies and learn more about the Bible and teachings of Jesus," Lawrence suggested.

"I agree," Jean replied. "So many things I have read in the Bible don't make much sense to me especially in the Old Testament. Maybe it's time to have some of it explained to both of us."

CHAPTER 68

Lawrence's year of Presidency passed by quickly and he managed to juggle both jobs really well. He decided to hold his convention at the Ritz Carlton at Laguna Niguel on the Pacific coast of southern California. It was a beautiful venue and rooms, meetings, and dinners had to be arranged for 450 members including 10 Past Presidents from the Liverpool Cotton Association and several personal friends from England. A band had to be chosen for the final dinner dance, but they decided to let James and his band Chum and the Frenzy start off the evening after dinner was served. It was a blast. Their music just blew the crowd away and everyone got on their feet and rocked. James was the singer and nobody wanted them to get off the floor and let the regular band come on. The disgruntled band leader from the hired band said to Lawrence, "You have to get these amateur kids off and let us play."

"These amateur kids are my son and his band and they'll stay on while everyone is enjoying themselves," Lawrence replied. They came on later in the evening by which time everyone was worn out so they only played for a short time. However, they didn't complain again, after all they were being paid.

Julie's fiancé from England had arrived and they decided to get married and both go back to live in England. A wedding was planned in the garden prior to the Convention so it had been nonstop for several weeks.

It had been a great year, but it was good to have some quiet time and get back to normal, whatever normal might be Jean thought.

Lawrence enjoyed getting out to play more golf and Jean and her friend Sue Ann signed up for tournaments at the tennis club. Sally now had a baby boy called Christopher and was expecting again soon, the family was growing and they were very proud grandparents. Baby Charlie was born soon after and there seemed to be plenty of reason to celebrate these two husky baby boys. However all was not well and the marriage was deteriorating rapidly. After a few months of trying to make it work Sally flew back home to California with the boys. She had been living with a completely impossible situation and there was no turning back. The empty nest was now full again and Lawrence and Jean enjoyed having them home in a safe and loving environment. Sally went back to Fresno State University to complete her degree and during that time became a strong Christian putting her life into God's hands for her future. Lawrence eventually bought her a small house so she could live independently and after graduating with her degree she started to teach at a school in Firebaugh.

CHAPTER 69

Jean's faith journey continued and the family all started to attend North West Church and got involved in some excellent Bible studies. Two books Jean had read, 'More than a Carpenter' by Josh McDowell and 'The Case for Christ' by Lee Stroebel had given Jean more understanding of the Bible and the life of Christ. Jen's mother, Susan, offered to take her through a program called the Timothy program which answered many of the questions she had about who Christ really was.

She was suffering with blinding migraines which had plagued her for many years, but recently they had become much worse. She made an appointment with a Neurologist and after his initial exam he put her on a new medication. That evening they were out for dinner and a candle was flickering on the table. A migraine started and she felt sick, but the pressure in her head became unbearable which was something new. Lawrence excused them and took her home and got her into bed. The pain was intense and she threw up several times.

Sleep was almost impossible but she dozed off in the early hours of the morning and when she woke up and opened her eyes she was completely blind. A thick heavy mist shrouded out all of her sight. She cried out to Lawrence, "I can't see!"

"Blink a few times," he said. "Maybe it's just sleep in your eyes." She blinked but there was nothing…she was blind. He rushed her into the Neurologist as soon as the office opened. "Don't worry too much," the Neurologist said. "These migraines can affect the sight sometimes and it will probably come back." He put her on a steroid for the pain which was unbearable and told her to come back in a few days. Her sight did try to return, but it was completely distorted. She was seeing flashes of coloured lights with no other vision. They worried the cause could be a brain tumor, but a brain scan came back negative.

Lawrence made an appointment for her with a Neurologist at Scripps Clinic in LaJolla in southern California but it was five weeks before she was able to get an appointment there. One night she sat on the edge of the bed in unbearable pain and cried out in desperation, "Jesus, help me, don't let me go blind…. I need you."

Two nights later she had a dream and it was about a bible verse… just the book number and verse, but not the words: 1 Corinthians 2: 4. When she woke up she immediately called Sally and asked her to look it up for her as she couldn't read.

"You are not going to believe this, Mum. I have my Bible open to that chapter and verse right now." She read her the words that were being spoken to the Corinthians by the Apostle Paul.

«My message and my preaching were not with wise and persuasive words but with a demonstration of the Spirit's power so that your faith might not rest on men's wisdom but on God's power." Jean's heart lifted as she tried to absorb this message. All the books and other religious teachings were all based on men's wisdom. This was God just telling her that it was a simple act of faith to put her trust in Jesus, His Son. This was what had been missing in her Christian journey and she took the leap of faith and accepted Jesus as her Lord and Saviour.

Lawrence had been going through the Timothy program with their friend, Pastor Jim. They met once a week for almost a year in his office until Lawrence finally understood the difference between being a cultural Christian and one who had a personal relationship with Christ. He also took a leap of faith and Jim baptized both him and Jean in the swimming pool at their home.

CHAPTER 70

Jean and Lawrence traveled down to La Jolla to visit Scripps Clinic. Despite the peace from her newfound faith, there had been no change in her eye condition. Arriving at the clinic she was taken to the Neurology Department to see a Neurologist who took one look at her and sent her straight to the Ophthalmology Department and the doctor there called in a second doctor to check her out. They were horrified, the pressure in both her eyes was 70 when normal pressure should be under 20. They diagnosed narrow angle glaucoma, a condition that can leave you blind within few hours or days if left untreated. She had already lost a considerable amount of her sight and they started treatment immediately to try and relieve the pressure. She was then sent back to Fresno under the care of Dr. Richard Mendoza who did iridotomy and trabeculectomies in both eyes, holes under the eyelids to release the buildup of the fluid which was pressing on the optic nerve causing her to go blind. Dr. Mendoza was an excellent surgeon who performed six more surgeries over a period of two years. He was both caring and encouraging as she passed through this very dark time and he managed to save 10% of her vision in one eye and 50% of her vision in the other eye. It was truly a God given miracle because she should have been completely blind.

CHAPTER 71

Things had become very bleak. Jean could no longer do her art, play tennis, and do the normal everyday things. However, there were some things that lifted her spirit during that time. Sally had moved on, she had met a young submariner when putting out her trash one day. He was her neighbour and was on leave. He asked her for a date and they started dating. He was redeployed again, but the next time he returned from his mission she was there at the quayside to meet him. They got engaged, then married, and had a gorgeous little girl who they called Bethan May. Tom was a good father to both Sally's little boys as well as his new daughter. Julie's marriage had broken down and she had gone through a very difficult divorce. She now had two lovely little boys called Miles and Christian and was a single mother. She decided to stay in England and worked at the boy's school. Lawrence brought them over to visit several times and it was such a blessing to spend some time with them. Jean had so much to live for a loving and supportive family, friends, and five beautiful grandchildren

Lawrence had decided to retire from major business and started his own business working from home. He called it Lawrence Preston Associates and they turned the upstairs room into his new office. The room was large and spacious enough for two desks for both him and Jean as she planned to be his assistant. James and Jen's friendship had blossomed into a love affair and after completing university they both became teachers and were planning to get married. They loved Jen and they had become close friends with her parents, Susan and David.

David's business was harvesting cotton with enormous cotton picking machines and he took them out on one of the machines to see how the cotton was picked. It was fascinating and had advanced so much from the days when cotton was picked by hand.

Jean's sight finally stabilized and she felt so thankful that she had enough vision to be able to function again. Maybe she could do some art again she thought, or was this just wishful thinking.

CHAPTER 72

How Great Thou Art Sculpture

"I'm going to take us on a trip to Hawaii!" Lawrence said. "It will be good for both of us and we haven't been able to go anywhere for so long." It was a great idea and the moment they landed on the beautiful Hawaiian Islands they felt the stress and anxiety of the past two years melting away. They relaxed on the beaches and swam in the warm, clear, green-blue ocean, enjoying special Hawaiian foods and having the occasional Mai Tai.

On Sunday they headed for a small church nearby. It was a good service and then the music of the hymn 'How Great Thou Art' began as a young Hawaiian girl walked onto the platform. She started to dance a hula, but it was different to any hula dance they had ever seen. It was full of reverence as she gracefully moved across the stage raising her hands in worship to God. Tears came into Jean's eyes somehow this expressed the feelings of her own thankfulness for the healing that had taken place. It was being expressed in dance… something that was so hard to articulate in words.

When they came out of the church after the service she approached the young girl's parents. Her thoughts had turned to the possibility of making a sculpture of her. This was the first time in two years that she had felt like doing anything. "Do you think that I could take some photos of your daughter doing this dance?" she asked. "I am a sculptor and it touched my heart. I would love to try and make a sculpture of her." On their return to Fresno, Jean created a sculpture from the photos she had taken and named it 'How Great Thou Art'. It was a tribute to God who had saved her sight. She was also able to take a replica of the piece and give it to the girl's parents in Hawaii where they placed it on their desk in a major hotel and would tell people Jean's story whenever they stopped by.

CHAPTER 73

The wedding day arrived for James and Jen and as family and friends gathered at the church it was a time to celebrate this very special day. Jen looked beautiful as she walked down the aisle followed by a team of nephews and their niece: two little ring bearers, Christopher and Charlie, and Bethan who served as a flower girl. The vows were said and as the newlyweds walked back together there were cheers and tears of happiness for them. As Jen took to the floor with her Dad for the first dance it was a special moment. He passed her over to James and as they circled the floor the music suddenly changed to Country Western music, Jen's favourite. The bridesmaids rushed out with a white cowboy hat and boots and put them on her and they started a line dance. Everyone started to join in it was so much fun and the happiest of weddings.

CHAPTER 74

"The World Rugby Cup is being held in South Africa this year," Lawrence said. "Would you like to go?" Jean didn't hesitate, knowing how many years he had played rugby and how much he loved the game.

"Of course," she said, "and maybe we could fit in a quick trip to a game park while we're there." They were soon on a plane and heading for Cape Town situated on the southern tip of South Africa where the Indian Ocean and the Atlantic met. Cape Town was famous for its Table Mountain shaped like a table which overlooked the town. They met up with some old rugby friends and went to the matches that were held in different parts of the country. They were with a great group of supporters for the English team and after seeing them win in the quarter finals in Cape Town they went on to the semi-finals in Pretoria where England were overrun by the Jona Lomu and the All Blacks, the New Zealand team. The matches against the Spring Boks were fierce, but still full of the camaraderie that rugby players always showed. Tensions were high as they sat in the Johannesburg Stadium for the final game between the Spring Boks and the All Blacks, the New Zealand team. It would be a very tight match and as they discussed the chances of South Africa winning before the game started they were all feeling excited. They heard the loud noise of an aircraft coming overhead and without warning it dived right over the stadium so close that they all ducked, it looked as if it was about to crash. It was a huge 747 SP aircraft with 'Go Boks' painted underneath and as it lifted its nose and flew upwards everyone in the stadium breathed a communal sigh of relief. It was definitely a unique if not very scary way of supporting the Spring Boks.

It was an excellent game fought hard by both teams, but South Africa took the cup. President Mandela came out to make a speech and the whole stadium erupted to see him pronounce the victory. It was so special to be there at the time that apartheid was finally being abolished... it was the start of a new era for South Africa. As they went out from the stadium onto the street an amazing scene was taking place. People of all colours were dancing and hugging each other. Cars were honking and there was a real sense of unity in the town. This African nation's win was icing on the cake. A movie called 'Invictus' was made of this event which happened in 1995, but Lawrence and Jean felt so honoured to actually have been there for this momentous occasion.

They decided to fly to Zimbabwe and visit the famed Victoria Falls before returning home. The Falls were spectacular and in full flow. As they walked the pathway the spray drenched them and suddenly a very large baboon with a baby on its back came walking straight towards them. Knowing that baboons can be very vicious and especially protective when babies were involved... they stood still. "Don't move and don't look at it so it won't feel threatened," Lawrence whispered. They froze as it came so close and walked calmly by them. Relieved, they continued enjoying the beautiful Falls. That evening as they sat on the veranda of the Victoria Falls Hotel they were treated to a magnificent sight. A huge moon rose over the horizon casting its full moonlight over the Falls causing an ethereal mystical glow to shine through the mist. It was an awesome and very special moment.

CHAPTER 75

T hings at home were changing again. Tom was posted to Hawaii and Sally was almost due to have her fourth baby which would now be born at the military hospital in Honolulu. Fortunately Tom was not out at sea on a submarine and would be based at home for the next few months. Sally started to get bad migraine headaches which were really hard for her as she couldn't take pain killers. She had been practicing the 23rd Psalm, "The Lord is my Shepherd…." to use during her labour pains and the baby was born very quickly just as the nurse left the room. He breathed in some amniotic fluid and couldn't breathe and was rushed into NICU, the Neonatal intensive care unit. They would not let her see him and she felt desperate. She tried to pray, but she was just in a panic. A black nurse came into her room and said she would take her to see the baby. He had wires all over him, but in his crib there was a small tract with the 23rd Psalm written on it. She glanced around the other babies but none of them appeared to have one. The nurse comforted her and let her stay for a short while and told her that she should not worry, her baby was going to be alright. For the next few days she and Tom were able to see him briefly and she asked about the black nurse that had taken her in initially as she wanted to thank her for her kindness. "We have no black nurse here and we never have," they said. "You must have been imagining it." Sally knew she hadn't and wondered if she had met an angel. Baby Tommy went home with a breathing monitor and became a healthy baby and a very mischievous boy.

CHAPTER 76

The church was organizing a trip to Israel which would be led by Pastor Jim and an Israeli scholar who would bring the stories of the Bible to life. Lawrence and Jean signed up, and this promised to be a truly special trip. Deanna their friend and travel agent had made their bookings and IGM International Group Ministries had put together an amazing itinerary for them to visit many of the places that Jesus and his disciples had lived 2000 years ago.

Their first stop was to a Kibbutz on the shores of Lake Galilee. Early every morning for three days they would go to the lakeside and have communion, sing hymns, and pray as they enjoyed the beauty of the nature around them. They went out on the lake in a boat visualizing the Biblical story of Jesus walking on the water when the storm came up. In Jerusalem they visited the Temple and the Wailing Wall and on to Masada, a high hill overlooking the Dead Sea. During the Jewish rebellion in 73-74 AD the Romans destroyed the Temple and survivors fled to Masada. As the Romans neared their stronghold at the hilltop, the Jews committed suicide rather than being captured by the Romans. They went to the Holy Sepulchre Church in the Christian quarter of the old city which claimed to hold the tomb of Jesus at the site where he was crucified, buried, and resurrected. The church was like a grand cathedral built over the top of the tomb. However, there was a second site called the Garden Tomb which had been discovered by General Gordon in 1894 which had been bought by Britain and was maintained by volunteers who came from around the globe and were joined by teams of local Palestinians and Israelis. The tomb was in a rocky crag which looked like an authentic tomb and was situated close to Golgotha, the place where Jesus was crucified. They were allowed to look inside the tomb one at a time and saw the slab where the body had been laid. There were peaceful gardens all around it where people could take time to reflect, meditate, pray, and softly sing an occasional hymn. There was always a debate about which tomb was the real one, but the Guide who took them round put it very succinctly. "It really doesn't matter," he said. "We know that the tomb was empty and Jesus had risen and was resurrected."

Many more sites were visited, including Bethlehem where Jesus was born. Out in the Negev desert one day they came across a group of traditional nomadic Arab Bedouins, who were trying to get their sheep to cross over the road towards them. Lawrence whistled and to their amazement the whole flock ran over to them. Their group all laughed and said he had missed his calling as a shepherd. The Arabs shook their heads in surprise and joined in it was a very friendly encounter.

There were many wonderful memories to take back with them from the Holy Land. Going to so many places mentioned in the Bible had really brought this to life for them. THis happened most when Pastor Jim was able to read the biblical passages in each place they visited. They had found both the Israeli and Palestinian people so friendly it was truly a treasured time to remember. Jean, Nancy, Pastor Jim's wife, Susan, and Deanna became very close friends. A friendship that continued over a weekly get together for coffee once they returned. They even remembered Jean telling them about how sad she had been when she left war torn England to go to Africa as a child and couldn't take her Teddy Bear with her. They took her to a shop called Build-A-Bear on her Birthday and bought her a bear complete with safari outfit and sunglasses.

CHAPTER 77

Lawrence was asked to become a consultant on the Board of the Cotton Company of Zimbabwe. He had so much experience of cotton in Africa and they wanted his advice on growing, marketing, and risk management. It would mean that he would be travelling to Board Meetings in Harare four times a year and he really looked forward to being able to help the company. Zimbabwe had been going through very difficult times during the rule of President Mugabe and poverty was rife throughout the country. One of the Board members talked to him about his brother desperately needing a wheelchair. Lawrence was able to help, but it also made him aware of the enormous need for wheelchairs in this poverty-stricken country as well as the rest of Africa and many other parts of the world.

He approached his Rotary Club in Fresno about the possibility of raising funds for a wheelchair project. This was accepted with enthusiasm, and Lawrence chaired the committee and researched how to have wheelchairs made and delivered to Africa. He partnered with a Charity called "Free Wheelchair Missions," who donated funds to organizations who were trying to raise their own funds. They were able to deliver many more wheelchairs than they had ever expected. It became his passion and Jean understood why when she went on several trips with him to see the transformation and absolute joy on people's faces who had never been able to stand up and walk. Many of them lived in thatched huts in African villages and could only crawl or be dragged outside. One woman who lived out in the bush in a small hut surrounded by nothing but dry dusty earth, two half-starved dogs, a pig, and chickens that looked more like birds was carried outside by her family. She was put in a wheelchair and was completely overwhelmed by tears and thankfulness for this wonderful gift. She had not been able to be outside and sit in the sun for years. Lawrence, Jean, and the Rotary members who were making the deliveries stood in a circle around her and they all sang a hymn. They left as the family were trying to get her back in the hut, but she strongly resisted, at last she had some independence. There were so many stories and they were able to take their granddaughter Bethan with them on one of the trips. The children in the various centers just followed her around clamouring for attention and she seemed to have a baby or toddler in her arms all the time. They were all laughing and giggling and so excited to see some of their little friends being put into wheelchairs. It touched her heart to see these children who had so little compared to children in the western world and yet could show so much joy at everything they were given.

CHAPTER 78

Jen and James were expecting their first baby, and soon the beautiful baby girl named Taylor Annabelle was born. The family were all thrilled with her and she was Lawrence and Jean's seventh grandchild. Lawrence had promised Jean when they left England that he would bring the whole family together each year so Julie and her boys, and Sally and her family, would come over during the summer for three weeks. This way the cousins would get to know each other. It worked out so well for them all and when Jen and James produced two baby boys, Tobin and Travis, they became the proud grandparents of nine grandchildren. As the children grew up they had so much fun during their time together. Activities were centered around the swimming pool and the kids organized themselves into teams and produced daring water shows in the pool. During these shows they would line up and show off their dives and funky moves as they leapt into the water often head over heels. Parents and Grandparents were invited to sit on chairs and cheer, clap, and boo as required. Susan and David, Jen's parents, would join them and helped by bringing in some food to supplement the endless, "We are hungry!" mantra. Long lasting bonds were formed by the cousins which have lasted despite them living in different countries.

How did they all grow up so fast and make their own lives? Well, this is the way of all things, and now the new generation, our grandchildren are making their way in the world.

CHAPTER 79

Both Jean and Lawrence started thinking about downsizing. The house and the garden was so large they thought if they could move to a smaller home with less upkeep they could spend more time in Cambria where they had a beach cottage. Evelyn, a friend of Jean's, called her one day, "Why don't you consider moving to where we are?" she asked. Evelyn and her husband, George, had moved to a lovely Senior Living Center called San Joaquin Gardens which was set in 23 acres of beautiful spacious gardens with flowers, trees, small waterfalls, and walkways all around. "Come over and have lunch with us and I'll show you around," she said.

They were treated to a delicious lunch at one of the three restaurants and took a tour to see the many facilities that the center had. There was a central building with a Concierge desk, a Theater, library, and two other restaurants. Another restaurant, the Bistro, was in a different building as well as a Gym, a swimming pool, and many other amenities. Evelyn took them to a large sunny apartment with an outside patio and close to them. "This would be perfect for you," she said, "and we would love to have you as neighbors." As lovely as it was they decided that they weren't ready yet to move into a Senior living situation, maybe in 3 or 4 years they might consider it, but not yet.

They left a few days later to go to Cambria planning to see some friends who were also going to meet them there. The house looked at its best, Pink Cecile Brunner were climbing over the wicker fence and the gate and geraniums in the window boxes were in full bloom.

After unpacking they headed for Moonstone Beach and their favorite restaurant, Moonstone Beach Bar and Grill, where they had lunch and then walked on the boardwalk overlooking the sea. It was a perfect day, and the cloudless sky was a brilliant shade of blue and the sun reflecting its rays across the waves cast what looked like a lighted path.

"It almost looks like a pathway to heaven," Jean said as they sat on a bench and breathed in the beauty of it all.

They were having a nap in the afternoon when Lawrence woke her up, "I think I have a problem" he said. "I can't lift up my right hand and my arm feels weak and numb." Jean reached for the phone immediately and dialed 911, this looked as if it could be the beginning of a stroke.

The ambulance arrived quickly and took them to Sierra Vista Hospital who soon confirmed that he was having a Transient Ischemic Attack (TIA) or in other words, a mini stroke. After several tests they put him on a baby aspirin and they released him telling him to go home and see his cardiologist. The numbness had cleared up and when their friends Pauline and Tom, arrived from their home in Carmel he was in good spirits and they were all able to go out for dinner.

"Looks like you dodged the bullet my friend," Tom said, "but be sure to get checked out when you get home." The evening finished on a high note, but later that night Lawrence woke up again with the same symptoms only a little worse. Again they headed for the hospital in an ambulance and they confirmed he was having another TIA. Once more of the symptoms went away they called their son James and he came with a friend and drove to the hospital to bring them both back home to Fresno.

CHAPTER 80

"This was a real shot across the bows," Jean said. "Maybe this was the message we needed to hear and we should probably make the move we were putting off and go to San Joaquin Gardens. With my eyesight continuing to deteriorate and you having these scares we would have the help there that we might need." Lawrence totally agreed and they signed up to purchase the perfect apartment that Evelyn had shown them.

Life became a flurry of activity as they prepared to put their own home on the market and make this final move. It was a monumental task turning out drawers and cupboards in the house and studio and trying to decide what to take with them and what to leave behind. They called on their friend Marsha who was a very talented Interior Designer and within no time she took measurements of essential furniture and pictures for the walls and drew up a plan for their new home. Everything started to fall into place and they were ready to make the move.

Jean woke up early on a Sunday morning and said, "We'd better get going if we don't want to miss church." There was no response so she switched on the light. "Wake up, Lawrence," she said, but he didn't answer. She realized that something was really wrong... he was struggling to speak, but no words would come out, he was having a major stroke and was paralyzed on his right side. She called for an ambulance and he was taken to Community Medical Hospital. Sally came over and the two of them followed him to the hospital where they put him on a gurney in the Emergency Room. They had to wait outside for 2 hours and then could only go in one at a time. The E.R. was packed with patients, nurses, and doctors and they set to work on him immediately. There were no beds available in the Neurology Ward and he had to stay in the E.R. on the gurney for two days and nights while they did numerous tests. He was not completely conscious and could not swallow or speak. Sally rang James who came straight to the hospital and when they rang Julie she said she would take the earliest possible flight from England and be with them.

Two days later he was taken to a room in the Neurology ward where the doctor informed them that he'd had a very serious stroke and that he may not make a full recovery. This was so hard to hear as he had always been so active and had always attended a Gym. Two Pastor friends, Jim and Greg, visited the hospital and started a prayer chain of people to pray for him.

A few days later he was sitting up in bed and when Jean bent down to give him a kiss he mumbled, "I love you." It was hardly understandable, but the first words he had tried to utter. They all gave him a thumbs up and the nurse decided to try and make him eat. He shook his head so she said, "Why don't you try he may take it better from you." There was apple sauce on the tray so Julie took the spoon at said, "C'mon Dad you can do this, open your mouth." He did and managed to swallow and suddenly tried to lift his hand and grab the spoon. Apple sauce went everywhere, but there were two hopeful signs, he was trying to speak and could swallow. Shortly afterwards they moved him to the intensive therapy floor where they worked on his speech, memory, and physical therapy. Forty days later after being sent on to another Physical Therapy Center he came home with no disabilities. The doctors were amazed. They rarely saw anyone come out of a severe stroke without major problems, but they hadn't recognized the power of prayer, it was truly a miracle.

CHAPTER 81

The move into San Joaquin Gardens went very smoothly thanks to Marsha who had even had the bed made up so that they could sleep there on the night of the move. They were made so welcome by Team members as well as so many of the residents who were very friendly. This was turning out to be the ideal place for them as Jean's eyesight had become really difficult. She no longer had to cook and they had excellent food provided for them. They signed up for a Yoga class and enjoyed some of the events that were available and made many new friends over dinner in the various restaurants.

Northwest Church was doing and event called "21 Days of Prayer" where people could go and pray in the church early in the morning. At the end of the 21 days they were going to do a Healing and Anointing Service with the Pastors and the Elders of the Church.

"I think I'd like to go to that," Jean said. "I am almost completely blind and we do believe in the healing power of prayer." Lawrence took her there on the Saturday morning and Pastor Will offered to anoint anyone who would like to have it. They moved into the Lobby outside the Sanctuary where it was quieter. Jean sat in a chair with Pastor Will and the Elders laying their hands on her shoulders and Lawrence standing behind her.

"What healing would you like God to bless you with Jean?" he asked.

"I would like to get my eyesight back," she said.

"Do you believe that God can do this for you?" he asked.

"Yes, I do.... but then I kind of go back and forth believing it," she said.

"Well, just keep that belief Jean, nothing is impossible with God if it is in His will," he said. They started to pray over her and suddenly she felt her whole body starting to shake uncontrollably from head to toe. She had no idea how long it lasted and she felt tears springing from her eyes when it stopped. They had all felt it and Lawrence thought she was sobbing but she wasn't.

Her eyesight hadn't come back, but she was left with a feeling of peace and joy and that God would take care of her whatever might happen. She had seen people being healed instantly on television but never believed it was necessarily true. For the next few months her eyesight continued to get worse and she could no longer find her way around their apartment. Lawrence took her to the Center for the Blind in Fresno and she started learning to walk with a white cane. At times she felt emotional but would pray to Jesus and always felt a sense of peace and comfort.

CHAPTER 82

Seven months later she went to Stanford Hospital for her usual check up with her glaucoma and cornea doctors. There was little hope of any improvement, the cornea doctor had previously said a corneal transplant was far too risky considering the glaucoma damage. However, this time he said he could attempt it. There was no downside as she had already lost her sight in both eyes.

"Think about it," he said. "There is no guarantee that this will make any improvement."

"When can you do it?" Jean said without hesitation. He had no openings for the next two months but he checked again on his computer and a cancellation had just come up for two days ahead. Lawrence left her in the hands of a nurse on the day of the surgery and she was told that she would have to lie on her back all night after she got home. She woke up after the surgery in the post op area with a nurse sitting beside her, she still had no vision. Lawrence picked her up after four hours and took her straight back to the Stanford Motor Inn where they were staying.

Lying on her back she and Lawrence both prayed for a miracle and by the morning their prayers had been answered. She was able to find her own way around the room and as the day went on she began to see colors, and although fuzzy, she could make out people and objects. Her heart overflowed with thankfulness as she was able to function once more on her own. Being blind had taken so much from her and she knew that this miracle of regaining her sight was God given.

CHAPTER 83

L ife is a journey of discovery with many different paths of twists and turns. It can take us to far distant lands where people of all different colors, creeds, and cultures reside. It is a privilege to be able know some of these people, who despite their differences, still have the same hopes and dreams that we all do. We live on Planet Earth created by the God of the Universe and despite the mystery of life itself we hope for love and peace as we travel this road during our life on earth. Throughout the ups and downs of each life there remains a thread binding us all together. We are family and treasure the love and memories we carry deep within us all.

ABOUT THE AUTHOR

Jean Preston was born in England and moved with her mother to East Africa as a young child at the end of World War 2. Her father was working for the British government who were starting to transition Uganda from a Protectorate toward their own self-government. Her school years were spent at boarding school in Kenya and afterwards she went back to England to pursue a career in Nursing. On her return to Uganda she met her husband, a young cotton merchant, where they married and had three children. As a family they lived and had adventures in many different countries and cultures before moving to the USA in 1980. When she moved to the United States her creativity bloomed and she began her new career as a sculptor. Her sculptures and other artwork reflected many of her experiences from childhood and put her on a journey to find the true meaning of her Christian faith.

Jean has always had a creative spirit and so when she had a sudden loss of eyesight her ability to sculpt was taken from her and she chose to turn to writing. This memoir represents her creative spirit as she tells the story of the different lives that she and her family have experienced.